MW01613762

KAREN CONRAD

7

SECONDS

The 7 Second Rule:
Why Your House Is Not Selling

Copyright © 2017
ISBN 978-1-54390-820-6

All rights reserved. No part of this book shall be reproduced,
stored in a retrieval system, or transmitted by any means—
electronic, mechanical, photocopying, recording, or
otherwise—without written permission from the publisher,
except for the inclusion of brief quotations in a review.

About the Author

Karen Conrad is the principal and owner of Karen Conrad Home Staging, where she has helped homeowners, real estate agents, and investors sell their listings quickly and at a solid price. She is also a marketing director, business and home staging instructor, public speaker, and real estate agent with 30 years of professional business and leadership experience.

In *7 Seconds*, Karen reveals the home staging system she created that has successfully moved real estate for her clients since 2013. *7 Seconds* is full of before and after pictures of homes she has personally staged so that you can learn how to successfully stage your own home or listing using Karen's proven system.

Karen Conrad lives in Colorado Springs, Colorado, and is from Minnesota, the beautiful land of 10,000 lakes She has a son, Levi, and was married to the late Tim Conrad.

To book Karen for speaking and consulting, contact us at **www.KarenConrad.net**.

Karen is on Facebook, Twitter, LinkedIn and Youtube!

  **Linked** in. You Tube

This book is dedicated to my parents, Larry and Betty Kruse, who have loved and supported me all my life. You are truly an inspiration to me and the best parents in the world.

About the Author   3

Introduction   6

Chapter 1 Karen's Secrets to Selling Homes Fast   10

  A. Make a Commitment   11

  B. Employ These Three Key Strategies   13

  C. The Importance of Staging In Our Modern-Day Home Industry   16

  D. Let the Detachment Process Begin!   16

  E. Treating Your Home as a Commodity to Be Sold!   18

Case Study 1   20

Chapter 2 Identifying Your Buyers   22

  A. Getting to Know Your Buyer   23

  B. Communicating with Your Buyer   25

  C. Drawing a Picture of Your Buyer   26

Case Study 2   28

Chapter 3 Preparing to Stage Your Home   30

  A. Where to Begin? It's Decluttering Time   31

  B. Communicating Each Room's Purpose   33

  C. Painting a Lifestyle with Product Placement   35

Case Study 3   38

Chapter 4 Staging Your Home: "Must-Stage" Rooms   40

  Must-Stage Rooms   41

  Kitchen   42

  Master Bedroom   46

  Dinette or Dining Room   50

Table of Contents

Master Bathroom   52

Living Room   55

Powder Room   57

Case Study 4   60

Chapter 5 Staging Your Home: Smart Presentation Tactics   64

    A. Creating an Updated Look Through Staging   65

    B. Repainting, Repairs, and Renovations   69

    C. Handling Design Blunders   70

Case Study 5   78

Chapter 6 Karen's Tips for Selling Your Home Fast   80

A. How to Keep Your Home Staged   81

B. Final Remarks: Karen's Tips for Selling Your Home Fast   84

C. How to Create the Best MLS Listing on the Market!   85

Chapter 7 A Re-design Case Study: SOLD to the First Buyers Through the Door After It Was Staged   88

Chapter 8 Before and After Photos: Vacant & Occupied Homes   114

Vacant Home Photos   116

Occupied Home Photos   170

Chapter 9 Bonus: How Not to Break the Bank   208

    A. My Top Choice Stores to Buy Inexpensive Décor   211

    B. DIY Designer Décor   213

    C. Creating a Christmas Look   216

    D. Chalkboard Coaster Feature – For Under $2 218

Chapter 10 Now It's Your Turn!   220

Introduction

There is something within all of us that craves transformation. Often we seek this transformation in our personal lives, our appearance, and our surroundings. This common desire is present in all human beings and is put in us by the Creator himself. It plays out in our everyday lives, helping us to seek a better way of living. This desire can also extend to include home decorating. Just think of what has happened so far with the introduction of Home & Garden TV (HGTV) several years ago. I talk to people every day who just cannot get enough of those products—and the allure of these programs is the before and after transformation of the home. This is the part I like the most about home staging. Seeing this transformation motivates people to seek something similar for their homes. As I go to homes that are getting ready to go on the market with no success, I am presented with a unique opportunity to bring transformation not only to the physical appearance of the home but also to the lives of the homeowners. As a home stager, I have seen just about every situation you can imagine when walking into people's homes during this critical time in their lives as I seek to help them transition from the home and make it market ready.

I am privileged and entrusted with the sacred role of entering into one of the most important, personal, and transitional times in people's lives. When you are moving people's most personal possessions in their home, replacing family mementos with new décor and guiding them through a decluttering process, you have asked your client to extend an incredible level of trust. I get a lot of satisfaction from helping people get the transformation they need in their homes. When I stage a home for a client, I do it with my heart. My reward is seeing the delight in the sellers' eyes because of how beautiful their home looks. They feel relieved because their home is presentable and beautiful for their future buyer, and the house goes under contract for a solid price that allows them to transition smoothly into the next stage of their life. As you read this book, my prayer is that you receive joy, hope, and an open door to transformation in your own home.

Chapter 1

Karen's Secrets to Selling Homes Fast

As a real estate agent and home stager, one of the burning questions I am most often faced with from my clients is "How do we sell our home faster for the best price possible?" I tell my clients that selling your home faster is possible and depends upon the level of commitment you make to selling your home. I then walk them through the practical steps of staging their home, which I share in this book. We will be identifying a fresh new way of looking at the owner's home that will position you for success. From a very broad perspective, homeowners are essentially transitioning into a new stage of life, and it is our job to help them do this as seamlessly as possible. By the end of this book, you will have my home staging secrets, inside information, and personal design tips that I consistently implement to bring success to my clients. The secrets I share will help you get your listings from "active" status to "sold" in the least amount of time and for a solid price.

A. Make a Commitment

You probably know from experience that home transitions can be an emotional time for the owner, so we must help our clients move on to the next stage and get focused on selling their home. Our goal is to find the right person to buy their house for the best price possible and for the owner to transition into a new and better home or investment they will enjoy. Helping your homeowner reach their goal and assisting them with any alleviation points in identifying a buyer and finding them a new home will make the process go by smoothly for them.

As their realtor, you are going to help the owner adopt a fresh new way of looking at their home from now until it gets sold. They will now be referring to "their home" as "their house," which is now for sale. A home is where an individual or family lives; a house is a commodity on the market to be sold.

As a home stager, what I would always emphasize to the homeowner and real estate clients I have worked with in the past is that home staging is a necessary step to sell your house faster for maximum profit. Furthermore, unless the real estate agent was also a home stager, the financial costs of hiring a stager and getting the house in *ready to be sold condition* would largely need to rest on the homeowner in some form or fashion. All of the homeowners, real estate agents, and house flipping professionals who took my advice have benefited from my staging efforts—many selling their homes, after previously sitting on the market for months, in six days or less. I myself still employ the home staging and selling strategies outlined in this book as a real estate agent, all to say they are a large value-add to the real estate process that <u>works</u>.

That being said, as the realtor, you will benefit from the strategies outlined in this book, and they will give you an edge in today's competitive market that will set you

14

apart from any other real estate agent. The more you put into the process of getting your listings market ready at the beginning, the more you and your clients will get out of the listing in the long run—or should I say short run. You and the owner will be joining forces to get the house sold, and the key sales strategies (including staging) I outline in this book require extra effort and costs that will pay off. Therefore, the owner must make a firm commitment to work with their realtor or home stager in following these practical steps so that they are in the best position possible to attract the perfect buyer. If the homeowner is willing to do this, they will be the right client for you to work with, and they will enjoy attaining their goal of selling their home.

B. Employ These Three Key Strategies

Did you know that the average homebuyer will decide whether or not to purchase their new home within the first 7–10 seconds of walking through the door? HGTV has made home selling especially competitive these days because of people's craving for transformation. As an agent, this means it is your job to grab the buyer's attention by making your house—their "home"—as neat and visually appealing as possible. Your buyer should be able to see something unique and interesting about your house that will make them want to stay.

The competitive nature of the real estate market should stimulate you to look at your house as a commodity on the market to be sold, which requires execution of three key sales strategies, all of which will complement one another. The first strategy is home staging. By creating a "staged look" for your property, you are showcasing it

at its fullest potential and helping buyers visualize themselves living in it—which will improve their chances of purchasing it. From a marketing standpoint, the way you stage a house can invoke feelings of comfort, passion, romance, and an edge that draws them to the home. Statistics have shown that houses that are staged sell faster than houses that are not staged because of this emotional factor. Our modern-day home industry consists of buyers and investors trying to get the best deal on their next new home or investment.

16

And like any other product, sellers (realtors) want to sell something competitive and intriguing for buyers.

The second key strategy to employ for a great selling experience is to ensure your house is competitively priced based on comparables, or "comps," in the market. Check the prices of similar houses in your area, and do an analysis to ensure you set the right price for your listing. Buyers always do comparison shopping among listings in an area to determine the best choice for their budget, and so should you. Remember not to undervalue your home, especially since you are staging it. A home that is staged will lend itself to receiving the best price possible for itself in the market. I have many clients who like to flip homes and who leverage the act of staging in the process. You can also look at staging as an ace in your pocket when it comes to setting the best price for your listing.

The third sales strategy to draw buyers into your house is to take great photographs of your listing. Buyers have to pick and choose the number of homes that they will physically go see, and you can use your photos to showcase its uniqueness, architecture, and interior design for your MLS listings in order to bring them to your door. The vast majority of buyers in today's market look for homes online, so making your best impression on the Internet is an extremely important part of the successful sales process. When you stage the home, it gives your photographer something to showcase. I encourage you to get a professional photographer with an eye for design, and ensure that they cover the details of the house that give it an edge. Your photographer can focus on aspects such as a pool, a garden, a spacious living room, or an antique staircase. I touch more on photographs in the last chapter of the book, but be intentional to showcase elements of the home that will hold the buyer's' attention while they are spending hours looking for their next home online.

DESIGN PRINCIPLE: What should I do with the owner's personal items? Put them in the garage or, if you have the luxury, in their new home. If personal items are stored away, this communicates that the owner is ready to go and serious about selling this home to the next buyer.

C. The Importance of Staging in Our Modern-Day Home Industry

For the buyer, looking at homes is shopping for homes, and you want to create a positive experience for them as they walk through the door. An effective way to do this is by appealing to their senses in the areas of touch, sight, smell, and hearing. You could bake some fresh cookies, which will bring a welcoming and comforting smell inside the house and could inspire pictures in a buyer's mind of creating memories in the home with their children, grandchildren, friends, and family. In addition, ensuring that the house is clean and free from dust goes a long way. Scents and cleanliness create lasting memories in the brain and will promote positive emotions in the heart of the buyer. If you can create a staged setting in your house for the buyer to see themselves comfortably living in, you have solved a major piece of the puzzle. This, coupled with a competitively priced house and nice photos for your MLS listing, will place your home perfectly in the eyes of the buyer within the landscape of today's real estate market.

D. Let the Detachment Process Begin!

In order for your and the homeowner's selling experience to be a successful one, it is necessary for the seller to firm up their commitment

Staging Stats: The U.S. Department of Housing and Urban Development found that staged houses have an advantage of 17% over unstaged houses in being purchased. The National Association of Realtors found that staging may cost 1% to 3% of the asking price, and this generates revenue from an 8–10% return. Homegain.com research shows that staged homes spend 83% less time on the market, basically showing that staged homes are bought faster than homes that aren't staged. A Coldwell Banker survey showed that staged homes are bought in half the time it takes to sell an unstaged house.

18

to detach from their home at the very beginning of the process. Sometimes one of the most difficult steps for a homeowner is to stop picturing themselves as the "owner of this home" and to transition to the "seller of this house." Transitioning to this mentality is important because it supports necessary steps to effectively prepare to market the home.

One of the first practical steps you will be taking with the homeowner is to remove any personal effects in the home. This is as easy as removing personal photos from the walls or the refrigerator. Our goal is to communicate to buyers that this home is open for purchase.

Seeing personal items in the house while walking through the house makes buyers feel uncomfortable, like they are "encroaching" on one's property. Therefore, a homeowner's firm commitment to detach from their home helps take "them" out of the house and put the new homeowner  in it—FAST. Another proactive step to take with the homeowner is to start looking for new properties. Focusing on "life after the sale" helps take the focus off their current property and also makes the negotiation process much smoother in the end. Why? Because sellers who are less emotionally vested in their properties are mentally prepared when offers start coming in. By making this committed decision to sell, your homeowner is choosing to welcome buyers in the door.

E. Treating Your Home as a Commodity to Be Sold!

Over time, homeowners and real estate agents have realized that marketing a listing in its current condition just isn't enough to receive top dollar for it. Putting a house on the market in "as is" condition, without putting the attention into it that it deserves, is like selling an item on eBay that has not been cleaned up or well-presented while expecting people to pay the same price for it as items that are nice and well-presented with great photos that showcase what is being sold. How well would that work out? On eBay, the strategy is to sell an item in its best possible state and then to take great photos of it so that it stands out above the rest, which yields the seller getting the best price for it that the market can handle. If an item is sold "as is" (not cleaned up or at least presented well), it will sit on eBay longer and will get the lowest price possible that the market can bare. These same principles apply for the real estate market.

The realtor's primary job is to present the house in the best way possible and to sell it for the highest price possible for the benefit of all parties involved. A realtor who can sell a house faster for the most profit is worth more for their services because they are able to sell a house commodity efficiently and effectively. For a realtor, the nicer the condition the house is in, the easier it will be for them to sell.

It would be quite a difficult task for a realtor to walk a married couple through an unkempt home and then have to try to convince them to buy it. The best practice for selling a home is for the homeowner and the realtor to work together to prepare the house to be sold so that the realtor can sell it quickly. The cost to do this will pay everyone back in dividends (see previous statistics).

Your goal will be to draw people to your house by presenting it well, especially in the MLS listing. Be ready to make some simple adjustments in the house décor to help the home appeal emotionally to the potential buyers. When house hunting on the Internet, people quickly weed out houses they are not going to visit. Buyers are not going to flock to your house and buy it right away just because they are in the market to buy a home—people need to be drawn to it. Many other houses are vying for their attention, so you as the realtor need to help the home appeal to the potential buyers and be the first property on their list to see. People do not have time to waste looking at unattractive houses, and if they do, they will ask for a price reduction because the perception is that this house has not been valued by its owners. People want to find their house quickly, so drawing people in the door with a nice presentation will get more showings, which positions you to sell your house faster because people will be moved to act quickly, knowing a beautiful home priced right is in high demand.

Preparing your house to be sold will require an investment of time and some money. Not every homeowner likes to hear this, but investing in staging does cost some money, although it will pay off when the buyer purchases the house. One way to justify the expense to your seller is to help them understand that investing in staging pays dividends compared to *not getting top dollar on your listing* or sitting on the market for months. With price reductions, homeowners part with tens of thousands of dollars by the end of the transaction, and so parting with some time and money to prepare your house to be sold in the beginning is an investment that will more than pay for itself in the future.

Chapter Summary

1. HGTV digital home shopping has significantly impacted the way we sell homes today.

2. The detachment process helps the homeowner focus on selling their home and mentally prepares them for closing the sale and negotiating with buyers at the end of the transaction.

3. Your house is a product that should be invested in. With time and a little bit of money, your house will be more profitable and will sell faster. Staging is **vital** for home profitability!

I got a call from one of the real estate agents that I work with, and I could tell that she had a problem on her hands with one of her listings and needed help from me fast. The home had been on the market for over 90 days, and there was no interest for several reasons. There were large dogs in the home, which means dog hair, and that plus the homeowner's mid-moving state was more than what potential buyers could see past.

The agent was faced with a stressful situation with this home: The sellers had found a house they wanted to buy but could not swing both homes, so they signed a contingent offer on the new home. In the meantime, there was interest from another buyer on that home, and all at once the agent had to figure out how to sell their existing home in two weeks or they would lose the new home. With 90 days on the market and no offers, it was time to make something happen!

The agent contacted me, and I went over to the home to see what I might be able to do to help get the home sold. I was presented with some real staging challenges. The home was a multi-level, and the entrance oddly came into the lower level where there was a mish mash of furniture and items half boxed up, a purple wall, and two spare bedrooms right in front of the entrance. Up a half a flight of stairs was the kitchen, dining, and living area, which was dark and with an odd floor plan to boot. Up another half a flight was the master suite with no doors for privacy, and the bed was right

Before

After

in front of the wide door opening. If there was an opportunity to be a little overwhelmed, this was it! Not only was the house oddly laid out but the dogs continued to shed, and I had two weeks to not only stage the home but help get a contract in place.

The results? I got the home staged, it went under contract within days, and the homeowner is happily in their new home!

Testimony of Sale

With two weeks to sell the home after being on the market for over 90 days with no interest or offers, it sold in a matter of days, allowing the home-owner to move to their new place and the agent to have a nice sale on a property that looked impossible.

After

Chapter 2

Identifying Your Buyers

Home buyers are attracted to particular characteristics in a home and its community. Identifying your buyer is important for you to be able to appeal to their preferences when preparing your house to be sold. Now more than ever, Americans are being served according to their tastes. This is a very important key to selling your house fast in today's market because people need to see what they want. We will be learning some tips regarding buyer identification and suiting their needs in this section.

A. Getting to Know Your Buyer

You can "get to know your buyer" by recognizing the most attractive characteristics of your house, neighborhood, and local surroundings. This key information will help you identify the most likely target market for your listing, understand why your house would be attractive to those buyers, and, finally, know what to communicate in your MLS listing and in person. Just a few characteristics you will be looking for are the average age, family size, and personalities of the homeowners in your area. This information gathering is as simple as observing who is currently living in your neighborhood,

what key attractions are in your community, and whether your sellers are "empty nesters" desiring to downsize from their large family home; buyers with families will be a natural target market to gear your marketing and staging toward. Therefore, you would want to highlight the number of bedrooms in the house, showcase the family theater room, and draw attention to the large back yard. Knowing this information allows you to stage the home in a family-friendly way to attract these buyers. Most buyers also prefer to go online to shop for houses, so noting information about the local trails, nearby convenient shopping areas, and schools are perfect details to add to your listing. In addition, showcasing any beautiful surroundings or house features in your MLS photos is another great way to make your house appealing for buyers. In the next few chapters, you will also learn *how* to capture great photos of the rooms in your house and which rooms are best to present online. All of these are concerted efforts toward intentionally attracting buyers to your house quickly.

B. Communicating with Your Buyer

Two chief ways of communicating with your buyers will be through your staging efforts and the information you present to your buyers online and at the property during showings. An example of how to communicate through staging, if your most likely target market is young military families, then using up-to-date, trendy colors with traditional furniture will appeal most broadly to this target market. Why? Because they often move here from all over the world, so it is important to use a decorating style that will appeal to all geographic areas. Often in Colorado there is an assumption that mountain decor will appeal to buyers, but that is not the case for people moving here from other parts of the country unless they are looking to specifically buy a mountain home. I rarely stage a home with a mountain theme unless it is actually a home in the mountains and a likely second or third home for the buyers.

As far as where you will be communicating to your buyers, studies show that over 95% of buyers do their initial shopping online. For those online, have the maximum number of professional photos loaded onto MLS. Doing the exercise mentioned in "Getting to Know Your Buyer" will help you identify the likely target market you will be attracting and helps guide what information you need to communicate with them. For example, if my target market is likely a buyer looking for a second or third home in the mountains, I will focus my photos and my description on the views of the mountains and the various ways they can enjoy mountain living at its finest.

C. Drawing a Picture of Your Buyer

Now you have the information you need to draw a picture of the buyers who will be attracted to your home. Start taking notice of the people living in the current neighborhood, and make a list of their characteristics on a sheet of paper. What do you see? Elderly couples, young couples, families with kids, or single people? Asking these questions will help you quickly identify your target market. From your list, you will be able to come to a general conclusion of the most likely buyers that will be interested in your house.

Next, make a description about what makes your house attractive to buyers using the information in the "Getting to Know Your Buyer" section. What is the size of your lot and the number of rooms in your house, what is the garage size, and does it have a beautiful back yard, nearby schools and conveniences, a family-friendly neighborhood, etc.? Again, this description will be used for your MLS listing and communications with interested buyers as well as information to guide your *staging*, which we will go into more detail on in the next chapter.

Chapter Summary

1. You can "get to know your buyer" by recognizing and understanding what the best characteristics of your house, neighborhood, and local surroundings are.

2. MLS photos are a great way to feature the best aspects of your house that you have identified will appeal the most to buyers.

3. Understanding your neighborhood community and their interests, and how those interests are met by living in that area, is key knowledge that will sell your house to your buyer.

One of my best home staging clients has a significant "fix and flip" business, and he recently purchased a manufactured home on two acres of land just east of Colorado Springs, which he asked me to stage. I had not staged many manufactured homes before, and I questioned his wisdom in purchasing and remodeling this home, as my expectation was that there is no market for this type of property. I drove out to look at the property to make a staging plan, and I realized that all the homes in the area were manufactured homes, which helped me to realize that there is a target market that desires these manufactured homes on the small acreage plots, and they are willing to pay almost as much for these homes as they would pay for a traditionally built home on a similar piece of land. This was an opportunity to learn about how to appeal to this target market through staging.

So I assessed the target market for this home and built a staging plan that would work well for a young family, possibly military. I accomplished this by ensuring that the colors I used were "in" and that the style would be slightly contemporary instead of heavy traditional to provide the greatest appeal to potential buyers that may have transferred in from another part of the country.

The finishes on a home like this are very basic. For example, instead of a real wood floor, they used a vinyl-based wood-look floor, and instead of high-end bathroom nickel or oil-bronzed fixtures, it had the basic chrome towel holders and faucets, which showed me that potential buyers looking for a home like this are expecting and probably comfortable with the basic finishing touches, so my staging needed to bring out the best of the home within the expectations of the buyer.

I used different colors with this home, such as turquoise accessories and complementary, bright-colored accessories to appeal to that younger buyer, and I was careful with the furnishings and the décor that I used for this home. In other words, I did not use the furnishings that I might use for a higher-end home in Colorado Springs as it would look out of place and make the buyer feel out of place. The whole idea of staging a home is to help the buyer see themselves living in the home, and if I used furnishings that I might use in a $1 million listing, the buyer might not see themselves living in that home, because it does not reflect their expectations of what their home might look like as they walked in or viewed it on the Internet.

The result? The home was sold for more than $10k above the original list price and was under contract in just a few days after I completed the staging.

Testimony of Sale

In just a few days after staging the home and uploading the pictures, the home sold for over $10k above the original list price and closed shortly after. Needless to say, my client is very, very happy with the results!

Chapter 3

Preparing to Stage Your Home

Now that we have laid the foundation for the importance of staging your house and getting to know your buyer, we are ready to discuss what it takes to make the necessary preparations to stage your home. Whether you or your clients are still living in the house or it is vacant, staging your listing might include a complete transformation or it could involve making just a few simple adjustments. Some of these changes will include making sure your house is in good repair. These repairs, if not completed, could potentially scare away buyers or give them the impression the home is not cared for, and the offers you receive on the home will most likely be lower in lieu of the expenses for repair they will expect to encounter. We will also be identifying some of the items or furnishings that could get in the way of effectively staging your house and finding a place to relocate or sell them. In this section, you will gain the necessary information needed to begin the preparation process of staging your home.

A. Where to Begin? It's Decluttering Time

Staging can be overwhelming, especially if you have a large house with several rooms to stage. So where do we begin? To make your staging experience easier, you must start by first decluttering the house. Decluttering can seem challenging, especially when one feels that everything in the house is relevant to living in the home or they are "treasures" in the eye of the homeowner that they see as valuable or contributing to the home. But once you understand the importance of detachment from the house, you will begin to identify the furnishings or items that seem to be crowding the space. Think of a Pottery Barn catalog: While some of the things in your house may hold precious memories for you, the buyer is interested in the look and feel of the home and does not hold the same sentiments toward your decorations that you do. When decluttering your house, choose to keep only the items that contribute to the catalog picture you want to give to the buyers that come through the door.

Before

After

One of the key ways to get through the decision-making process of what to declutter is to follow the rule of depersonalization: If it is personal, take it out, unless it adds to the overall feel of the décor. While you browse through your possessions, you are picturing how the item would appeal to an outsider as part of the overall look of the house. You will soon begin to notice things that should be put away, such as personal photos, mementos, refrigerator magnets, children's drawings, or even some old dishes.

The idea of boxing your household items may seem taxing at first, but it is a helpful component in the staging process. And with correct labeling and storage savvy, you will have an easier transitioning time in the end. Storing your boxed items in the garage is a great presentation tactic that shows potential buyers you are committed to selling your home fast!

One question that comes up from some homeowners is if their boxes are in the garage, what if people can't see what the inside of the garage looks like? Rest assured, as far as the buyer is concerned, what they need to know about the garage is whether their items will fit in the garage. If you can give the garage measurements, they will be able to gauge—even with the boxes—if it will serve its purpose for them. Our most important concern is preparing the home to be staged for your buyer, so boxing up your personal items and finding a place for them to be stored, like the garage, is an essential part of the process to get your home looking stage ready.

B. Communicating Each Room's Purpose

Each room represents the total functionality of the home. As we drill down a bit more, when the buyer walks in the door of any room in the house, he or she should be able to see with their own eyes the purpose of the room *hinting* at them with the decorations you chose.

Homework Assignment: Write down what you believe is the purpose of each room in your listing. Then think of how you might want the buyer to feel when they walk in the room. For example, I would want a buyer to feel warm, comfortable, and cozy in the living room. The purpose of this exercise is to come up with some decorating ideas based on how I want the buyer to feel, so I might decide to decorate the sofa with a few warm-colored soft pillows and a throw blanket. A candle on the coffee table with a rich apple cinnamon scent would add warmth and coziness through both sight and smell.

This is an extremely important concept in order to stimulate the imagination of the buyer so they can see themselves living in your house. You can do this through furniture and decoration placement throughout the room, just like a catalog.

For example, in the kitchen, you may set out a decorative bottle of olive oil—something that has to do with the action of cooking to make the kitchen come alive to the chef at heart. In order to illustrate the impact of communicating the purpose of a room to the buyer, the

35

kitchen is a real deal breaker for the cook of the home. How the kitchen looks and feels will be the deciding factor for them.

In fact, most buyers will bring their family to the showing, all of whom will be looking for certain aspects of the home that will be important to them. Each of these members will desire to see their favored area in a pleasing condition before giving their approval. Communicating each room's purpose through staging is one of the most important strategies used to attract the buyer to help them envision themselves living in the home.

In some cases, there may be rooms in the house that are practically undefinable, meaning, you are unable to identify the purpose of the room. In instances like these, staging is crucial to be able to paint a picture of the room for the buyer. Furthermore, there may be normal elements of a room that are missing, such as proper cabinet space. In this situation, it may be wise to develop the complete functionality and purpose of the room through furnishings and décor.

By defining the room for your buyer, you are taking away any doubts or questions in their minds that would prevent them from purchasing it. You can style and define each room of the house to act as a template for the buyer once they acquire it, thereby increasing your chances of selling it faster.

C. Painting a Lifestyle with Product Placement

Creating the feeling of a certain lifestyle through product placement is a marketing technique you can use to spruce up your home for the buyer with any brand name products you might have. As previously mentioned, getting to know your buyer will help you determine the type of buyers who will most likely purchase your house.

The point is to place things in the house that are appealing to buyers. When they see things they would buy, this just adds to the attractiveness of your house. This is as simple as putting Coach or Christian Dior shopping bags in some of the closets to portray a "shopper's lifestyle" or by putting a Keurig, Vitamix, or KitchenAid in the kitchen for those who use or like higher-quality kitchen items.

How to Choose Your Color Scheme and Foundational Design Elements of the House

1. Start with a design board, which includes:

   > three primary design colors that you use throughout the house and two complementary ones that you can use to add pops of color and interest in various rooms, as well as accents like pillows, accessories, artwork, and more.

2. I choose the materials for the tableware that provide interest but work within the color scheme.

3. Decide what your "one thing" is for that house, meaning the item that you build your decor from—the one item that you know will make all the difference in the house or individual rooms.

   > For example, if you have a home with a beautiful floor-to-ceiling stone fireplace, you may choose a pair of antique skis to lean up against that fireplace to provide a theme and add character to build your design around.

Creating this sense of a desired lifestyle through product placement is what buyers need in order to feel at home in their heart with their own preferences and aspirations.

DESIGN PRINCIPLE: If you don't feel comfortable putting a designer purse in your closet, try using a designer shopping bag instead—it still communicates the class that buyers want to see in their closets!

Chapter Summary

1. Preparing to stage your home begins with decluttering, which is an important process to remove personal items from the house.

2. By staging, we are transitioning from a personal preference of style to an accommodating sense of style for buyers.

3. Each room should communicate its purpose through the décor chosen.

4. You can appeal to your buyer's wants and desires through the product placement technique.

One of my greatest joys in staging is when I am called in to help sell a home that has been on the market for a long period of time with no results. Such is the case with this home!

After being on the market for 214 days, the homeowners decided it was time for a change, so they switched realtors, and the realtor gave me a call to stage the home. Some of the challenges I saw with the home that I could address with staging included significant square footage with all the same paint color and light carpet that seemed cold and uninteresting, dated parts of the home that were obvious when the home was vacant, and several other listings on the same street and within a couple blocks that we were competing with in a similar price range.

After I staged the home, it was listed at $10k more than it was just a couple months before with no staging. This home went under contract in 34 days with the higher price! The realtor and homeowner were very happy with the results.

Testimony of Sale

After being on the market for 214 days, the homeowners decided it was time for a change. After I staged the home, it was listed at $10k more than it was just a couple months before, with no staging. This home went under contract in 34 days with the higher price!

Before

After

41

Chapter 4

Staging Your Home: "Must-Stage" Rooms

When staging your home, there are some "must-stage rooms" that are most important—that every buyer will want to see. These rooms include the kitchen, master bedroom, master bathroom, living room, powder room, and dinette or dining room.

Knowing the rooms that are the power influencers in your home will help you stay focused on staging. It will help you create the right environment to ATTRACT the attention of buyers and to hone in your resources toward these areas. This atmosphere of attraction acts as a lure for the buyers to want to live in your house.

As always, make sure the "palette" you are painting on in these rooms for the buyer is clean, as previously discussed in the decluttering section. In this section, we will be learning how the room should "feel" to the buyer by appealing to their senses of smell, touch, and sight. You will be learning the fundamental practicalities on "how" to stage these rooms in order to get your home sold faster!

Must-Stage Rooms

The must-stage rooms of the house should always be staged and ready to be seen by potential buyers. Their best qualities should shine through the room, and they should be appealing. Here is your opportunity to make the most out of each room to get your home sold!

We will be focusing on the following concept in this section: When walking into a room, start gauging how that room makes you feel. If there are any inclinations toward negative emotions, you will learn to stage your way out of that emotion with the use of texture, color, and décor.

You will start to see how cold rooms can become warm through soft materials, warm colors, pictures, and the simplicity of greenery with strategic placement. Follow this principle through each of your must-stage rooms, and you will be able to stage them with success based on the feeling you get when you step into the room!

Kitchen

The kitchen is said to be the place where memories are made, or the "heart of the home." You can create a sense of warmth and hospitality in the kitchen through the décor, colors, and textures you choose. Simple is best in the kitchen because a good presentation of food requires space, and you are going to provide this for the buyer. The color scheme you choose also plays a role as you do not want a dull and boring kitchen but rather one that has some "pop" and depth.

Here is a 6-step checklist on how to get started with staging the kitchen:

1. The first thing you want to do in the kitchen is to create a clean and open space. Clear all the countertops of any clutter, not only for sanitation purposes but to create a clean palette for the future cook of the home. When buyers come into the kitchen, they are inherently thinking, "I will be cooking and baking cookies on these countertops"—so they want to see tops that are nice, neat, and clean.

2. Get rid of all the old dishes by keeping them stored away, and showcase your nicer ones in plain view in the cupboard. Never leave a dirty sink, and be sure to stow away dish soap and any scrubbing utensils.

3. Another way to keep the kitchen looking nice and neat is to keep the trash can out of sight and to the side, where people's attention is not easily drawn.

4. You can also remove any items on top of the kitchen cabinets as this can be perceived as a place collecting dust and clutter. This is also a technique I use to keep the eyes of the buyer off the ceiling and onto to the home's granite counter tops, appliances, etc. The nice, clean space will be pleasing and will be noticed by the buyer.

5. Create as much light as possible in the kitchen to portray the warm and inviting feeling we are going for. Change all the bulbs that are not working.

6. Again, touching on clutter, remember to look at the refrigerator, and remove any personal items, such as magnets, pictures, or sticky notes. Even if you have some wise words or pretty magnets, put them away because the buyer wants to see clear space that he or she can put their own memories on.

Each of these tactics helps maintain the open, clean, and inviting feeling the buyer desires to see in the kitchen.

For decorating, there are a myriad of things you can do to make things look clean and inviting. Here are seven steps you can take to begin the decorating portion of staging the kitchen:

1. After you have created your clean palette by decluttering, take a step into the room as an outsider; look at the kitchen, and evaluate some of your impressions of how it makes you feel.

2. Document them, and after reviewing your responses, address the negative items, and see what you can do to simply "fix" that into something positive. For example, if your kitchen feels a little "cold," consider putting some plants or flowers on the table to warm things up with a little bit of life.

3. For the countertops, you can cluster decorative or essential items together rather than having them spread out from the beginning to the end of the counter.

DESIGN PRINCIPLE: I always use simple, black round placemats (you can buy these at Walmart for under $5 each) and create clusters of décor so that the buyer's eyes will pleasingly bounce across the room just the way I want them to see the home.

4. If there are dark spaces under the counters, I add a small lamp, which makes it look really inviting, or you

can purchase battery-operated puck lights with adhesive that you can place under the cabinets to give it a look of having under cabinet lights.

5. You can also enhance the buyer's impression of the kitchen by adding a baking smell as they walk in. Fresh baked cookies are the best, but natural ornaments also work, and add the sweetest, most natural scent to the home without having to bake fresh cookies all the time.

6. You can also stage the kitchen to draw the eyes of the buyer to what you want them to see. For example, some galley kitchens, in my opinion, are far too narrow. In these cases, I place clusters of items to guide buyers' eyes through the room.

7. I also like to create eye-catching table settings in the room for guests to feast their eyes upon if there is a dinette space in the kitchen.

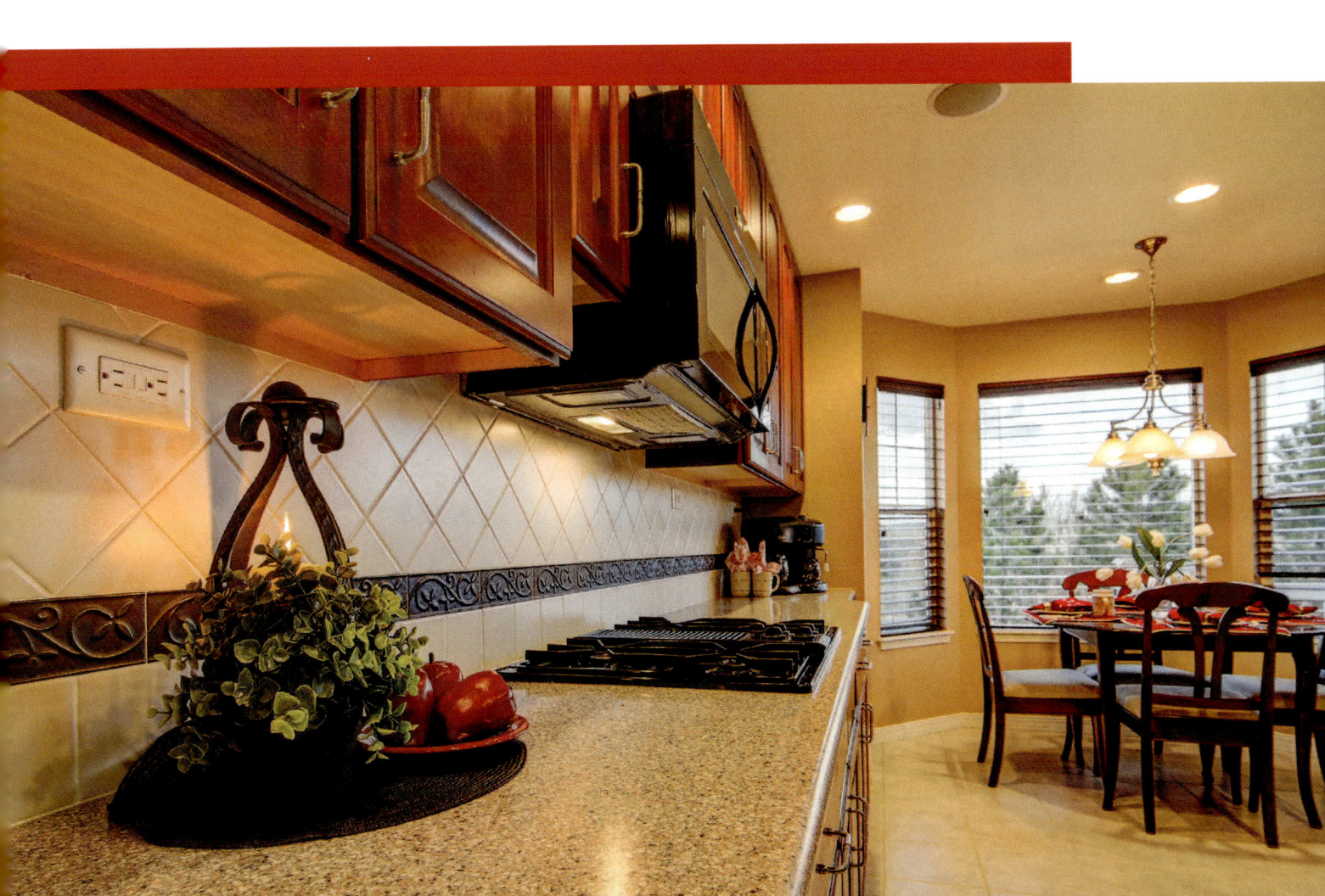

All of this helps to create a cleaner, more organized, designer look that will be pleasing to the eyes of the buyer.

Staging is a great way to guide people's eyes off of what you don't want them to focus on and onto what you do want them to focus on—which are the BEST parts of the room.

These small tips to decorate go a long way in creating that clean and inviting setting for your buyers in the kitchen.

Master Bedroom

The master bedroom is an important room that should convey comfort, luxury, and romance. The buyer should be able to see themselves settling down in the evening and being able to relax and rejuvenate. This is one of the rooms that should be totally depersonalized.

Here are 10 steps for staging your master bedroom:

1. Store away personal effects and personal artwork, unless it conveys the feeling you are trying to express in this room.

   You will be removing any sign of nightgowns, robes, photos, makeup, and books—unless, of course, you are trying to make use of one of these items, such as a book or perfume, as a decorative item to match your theme of décor or as a product placement item. In fact, the master bedroom should have no personal items at all.

   The buyer should not feel as though they are invading your privacy through the personal items inside the room.

2. In terms of furniture placement, there are a few techniques you can use. Try placing the bed at an angle for vacant homes in order to create something more spacious and more visually appealing. You could also try adding some

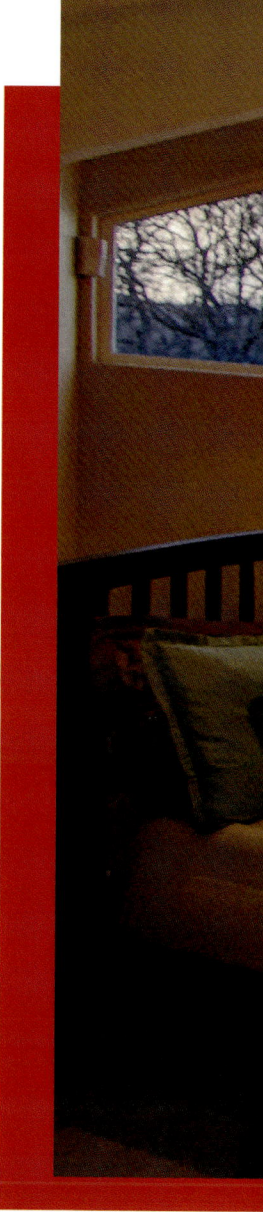

DESIGN PRINCIPLE: Go to Ross or Walmart and purchase a new comforter set for as little as $30. If you don't want to invest in a new comforter set, you can purchase a white duvet cover for your comforter and add some white pillows. For a special touch, add a vase of white flowers, such as lilies, in a vase next to your bed to complement the white bedspread, which adds freshness and elegance.

seats and tables so that a large master bedroom does not feel so empty.

3. The bed should be made neatly, and the covers should look new or luxurious.

4. To add a dramatic splash of color, simply add some decorative, colorful pillows to the bed over the neutral or white bedspread, then tie that color in with the flowers you choose, drapery, artwork, and/or accessories.

49

DESIGN PRINCIPLE: When you are decorating the master bedroom, make the design style a good balance so that it is not too feminine or masculine. Err on the side of femininity rather than masculinity if having to make a choice to ensure it communicates romance and elegance. Through your design, you can actually inspire the buyer to be able to visualize their décor inside the room. Nice, neat, clean, and depersonalization are key here for the buyer.

5. You may want to add a throw to the foot of the bed to tie it all together.

6. You could use linen spray or scented candles in the room to keep it smelling beautiful. You can find some of these items at your local dollar store, and the small investment will yield maximum benefit. These atmospheric solutions will contribute to the sense of fresh beauty that should emanate from the master bedroom.

7. Be sure the master bedroom has a nice, fresh, clean scent and is well aerated so that it does not smell stuffy.

8. Make the room feel open and bright, and let in as much natural light as possible.

9. Flank the bed with lamps to create softness and coziness. Light does wonders, especially lamps with soft white light bulbs. Changing the lighting of the room is a great technique to add brightness or to create a romantic feeling for the room.

10. The bedroom should be extremely clean—be sure to get rid of any old bedding or rugs in the room. Dust and clean every part of your room and furniture.

Dinette or Dining Room

The dining room is the place to create an entertaining setting for friends and family. In this room, we want to create an inviting, elegant

DESIGN PRINCIPLE: When setting up the flowers, go for a monochromatic look. Pick one color for the flowers so that it does not conflict with the style of the room. Monochromatic flowers also make the room appear neat.

atmosphere for the buyer. This can be done largely through décor, simple dramatic florals, place settings, and overall presentation on the dining table. You can create a decorator look with just about any table, no matter how old or what design. Whether or not you use a tablecloth depends on the style of the room and how the table itself looks. If the table has a beautiful, polished wood finish, you can maximize the beauty of the wood with a simple runner.

You will notice in the pictures of homes I have staged, when I use a tablecloth, I generally scrunch it to create more texture and interest to the setting and then place the chargers and plates strategically on the table to create a balanced look and feel. I like the "imperfect" look that scrunching provides to the table; it is formal yet not stuffy, creating a look that is inviting and comfortable for the potential buyers to linger while imagining entertaining their guests.

If you have an older table with a poor finish or some damaged areas, you can strategically place the tablecloth and place settings to avoid having those areas visible to those viewing the home.

This probably goes without saying, but make sure the room is clean, free of dust, and well lit. A dusty dining room leaves the impression with the buyer that the home is old and/or cold and uncared for, which is not what we want to convey to our buyer.

Another creative technique I use is finding some framed flower photos or paintings that complement the color and style of flowers I put on the table or vice versa. This makes it look like everything was carefully crafted and created just for this home and space and plants the seed in the minds of the buyers that the seller is meticulous with the home, which puts them at ease regarding the upkeep and maintenance of the home. This is subtle but just the kind of tips and tricks I have learned that help sell houses!

Of course, scented candles add a final touch to any dining room table. A safe color to go with for the candles is an undertone that you may find in the room. A bold color may be too much. In addition, dining room gems, such as higher-end collectible tea sets, wine bottles, etc., are a nice finishing touch for the room when you have a buffet table or decorative cabinet to display lamps or collectibles that complement the room. When deciding whether or not to display an item, stick with the rule of thumb that less is more. Simple decor will complement a nice, clean, open room to create the inviting, elegant feeling we are looking for.

In the DIY section at the end of the book, I show you how to create your own designer napkins. You can select material that goes perfectly with the décor theme of the home and very inexpensively create a custom look. Also, if making a runner, consider using tapestry material to provide your potential buyer with a rich, unexpected look. The key with using tapestry for the table is to choose material that has a mixture of complementary colors and textures that will provide the foundation for an elegant table. The last thing you can do is add that nice, dramatic, slightly oversized centerpiece, with a substantial vase and monochromatic florals, to make a confident statement about the beauty of the home you have for sale. In a small dinette, always remember that if you have too many items, it may start to feel crowded and unattractive—our goal is to stage it in an entertaining and inviting way.

Master Bathroom

The master bathroom is a great room to capture the interest of the buyer with décor and accessories that help them imagine relaxing in a spa-like atmosphere. While buyers will spend a lot of time looking through the other rooms, oftentimes buyers feel uncomfortable about being in people's bathrooms. It's just so personal! You will need to impress the buyer in the few seconds they spend there and grab their attention so they will want to stay longer.

Because it is a space heavily used by the seller in a very personal way, it is extremely important that all personal items are removed for a showing and that you have a plan in place with the sellers on what needs to be put away.

Here is a list of three things to get your master bathroom ready for staging when the homeowner or tenants are still living in the home:

1. The bathroom needs to be completely decluttered. You or your clients may not be aware of how crowded the bathroom is because they live there, but think about removing all the products you use in the bathroom, even the loofahs and daily use towels.

2. Any bathroom rugs on the floor should be kept away as well as I personally think they spur the buyer into imagining someone

A QUICK TIP:
I suggest to sellers that they have a clothes basket or other container designated to put all their personal belongings in right before a showing; then they can easily pack it up and bring it back out after they leave. This has worked well for clients!

else's feet using the bathroom. (Maybe this is just me but better safe than sorry!)

3. Clear the medical cabinet of any pills and prescriptions.

Staging the master bathroom will involve adding some flowers and also adding some photos or pieces of art to make it look stylish. For older houses, adding some subtle changes to the bathroom can make it look more modern.

Choose the color of towels that will look best in the room. For a clean look, go with white towels. For dramatic impact, go with red towels. For an elegant look, go with a black-patterned towel. If at all possible, carry the same color scheme from the master bedroom into your master bathroom; it will add to the designer look and feel for the buyer.

DESIGN PRINCIPLE: How high should I hang my mirrors or pictures? The general rule on a bare wall with no furniture underneath is 60 to 62 inches from the ground. If you have a taller picture, you can move it down around four inches at the most. If your picture is hanging above a piece of furniture, the general rule of thumb is to hang it five to ten inches above the top of the furniture. If you want to hang it above a fireplace or a mantle, three to six inches above the top of the mantle is the way to go!

Adding some candles makes a big difference, and it creates a romantic and warm feel to this very important room. You can add a candle to either side of the mirror, or you can mix up the height sizes of the candles. If the bathroom is large, think about improving the lighting in the room, if needed.

If you want to play up the spa experience, put up a white robe, and add some sea accessories near the tub or shower. The mirror should be clean and reflect the great lighting and various staging items you have on display!

For bathrooms with soaking or jetted tubs, I often add champagne glasses and a bottle of non-alcoholic champagne to help the buyer imagine their relaxing bubble bath in their new home.

TIP: For an older bathroom, leverage the power of black and white.

Living Room

The living room is the primary room of the house for entertaining and visiting with friends and family. It should convey comfort, softness, and a spacious, welcoming feeling for all that enter the home.

In this room, the buyer needs to be able to see themselves relaxing and being able to have memorable conversations with friends and family. Also, this will be the room the Christmas tree goes in, so if you have your listing or home on the market near the holiday season, be assured that will be on your potential buyer's mind as they are looking at homes.

The buyer also wants to know whether all their furniture will fit and, if not, if the room is big enough for them to make it work with some of their furniture and/or purchasing new while still feeling comfortable with their guests.

In staging, this is the most common room that should be depersonalized from the unique character and taste of the house owner, including family photos. Sometimes the owner's taste may be too unique for the buyer, so the rule of thumb here is to stay more traditional with a few pops of color. Floral decorations are safe and so is a look like Pottery Barn.

Furthermore, check to make sure the walls are free of minor graffiti marks and that they look clean. In terms of décor and furniture placement, the living room is the most important room to take care in staging because it will form a template for the buyer to see how they will arrange their own furniture to fit the room. It can be a deal-breaker but can be overcome by finding the most space saving and open arrangement as you can to convey that nice, welcome, and comfortable feeling the buyer is looking for.

The living room is a fun one to enhance and create positive emotions for the buyer. A tried and true way to make the room grab the attention of your buyer is to throw in some colorful pillows, particularly red pillows. Then include other accessories, such as artwork and flowers.

The artwork should blend in with the general feeling of the room and accentuate it. If you do not want to clash with the already set color theme of the room, black and white photos or paintings are an excellent way to go. You can also paint the walls to change the style of the room, but this is not necessary if you create your color palette with pillows, artwork, and curtains. Using warm colors when staging sends the buyer's heart racing and helps them see themselves relaxing in the living room.

Add a pair of plants on either side of a fireplace to soften things up, or use candles on the fireplace to give it a romantic feeling. Lastly, enhancing the lighting in the living room is very important and will make the room appear bigger, brighter, and more comfortable.

Powder Room

The powder room is a great opportunity to make a dramatic statement in your home with a small space. Generally, the powder room needs to look clean, elegant, and to the point—meaning, you want to keep things nice and simple. You want people to walk in and say, "Wow, what a cute powder room!"

The powder room is small with a high ceiling, which is why you want to draw people's eyes to the center of the room. The modern and preferred powder rooms have a raised sink that looks very elegant. If you don't have a raised sink, look at your present sink or cabinetry, and see what sort of impression it leaves with you in order to determine if it needs some enhancement, like a tall vase of flowers or soft, nice hand towels.

In addition, buyers prefer a powder room that is modern or one with character. Taking some of these variables into consideration will help you prepare a nice, clean slate to work with! Some very simple changes can be made in this room to make it stand out with a designer look.

You can have a large mirror with lighting on either side and then add some bold or bright colors to the center with flowers, a pretty soap dispenser, and a hand towel with a color that demands attention.

To choose the color of the hand towel, look at the flowers and soap dispenser that you chose to complement each other, and see if there is a small color that can be drawn out from one of those two items that will tie everything together.

A basic necessity that may go without saying, but is too important not to ensure you think about it, is a nice, clean sink. Something as simple as a stray hair in the sink can turn the buyer off. Put "clean powder room sink" on your checklist of items to do to get ready for a showing. I use Lysol wipes or something similar as they pick up dirt and leave a fresh scent.

As far as the look of the cabinetry and sink, if the two are rather old and rustic, with no particular elegance or niceness about them, you can fix that. In order to offset any glumness in the cabinetry, you could place a tall, dramatic, and monochromatic vase of flowers on the countertop that demands attention from the eye. This will become more dominant than the dated fixture and will keep attention off features of the home that do not provide a positive contribution to your listing.

An easy and inexpensive tip for a dated bathroom is to replace an older mirror by finding a reasonably priced one with some character at Lowe's or Home Depot. If you want to go the extra mile, think about doing some inexpensive faux finishing to the cabinetry and/or getting

DESIGN PRINCIPLE: Add an elegant lighting effect to your powder room with the use of some beautiful candles! These can be placed below the mirror or on top of the toilet.

some pretty handles or knobs on the cabinets to spruce things up. Some of these options will be an investment toward the sale of your house. However, staging will make a difference on its own just by investing in smart staging, and I have been able to help sell home after home with dated bathrooms using these techniques.

After all, research shows that people who stage their homes can actually get market value for their home or even up to 10% more. Adding a little bit of character to these rooms will draw buyers' attention and lure them to purchase your house faster!

Chapter Summary

1. You now know how to stage the various rooms in your house, from the kitchen, living room, master bedroom, and dining room to the master bathroom and powder room.

2. A good principle to follow in staging is to ask yourself how the room makes you feel and to stage your way into creating positive feelings about the room.

I receive calls from realtors and homeowners that have had their house on the market for months, sometimes a year, with no offers. This is really a difficult time for these home-owners as their house that they loved and lived in with their family is sitting vacant for months and the mortgage payments and taxes continue to have to be paid.

Such was the story with a recent home I staged near Colorado Springs, CO. The homeowners changed real estate agents because their house had been on the market for months with no interest, and the new agent immediately called me to come and look at the house. The home is in a nice neighborhood, and as I drove in, I saw there were several homes for sale on the same street and within a couple blocks. When I see that, I know that we will have to make this house stand out from the rest to ensure potential buyers in the area choose us.

I learned that the family transferred to the East Coast, they have six children (including triplets), and their house had been on the market for over 200 days with no offers. In addition to that, the house they were living in on the East Coast had had a fire, so they were faced with moving until that was renovated and still had this house in Colorado. I really wanted to help this family!

As I walked into the vacant home, I immediately saw that it was a nice home, but it felt very cold due to it being vacant, the light walls, the light carpet, and it having lower-end trim and finishes in comparison to the square footage.

I purposefully and deliberately study homes I stage through the eyes of a buyer, and nothing in the home

Before

After

drew me in to look at more. It did not feel like a home; it felt like a large, empty house where every flaw jumped out to greet me. (That is what happens when you walk into most vacant homes; the eye has nothing else to look at but the flaws.)

Here are five strategies I used to sell this home:

1. The unique round entry was beautiful, but light floors and light walls made it feel cold, and there was nothing that drew you into the home. I brought in a black oriental-feel rug to bring in elegance and ground the space and systematically placed artwork on the walls in a way that drew the buyer into the rest of the home.

2. I used red with black and white in the large powder room that was close to the entry of the home with towels, artwork, and florals. I added an ivy plant on the commode to ensure I had something natural with texture in this cold space. A dated bathroom suddenly looked sharp, up to date, and warm—just what a buyer wants their guests to experience.

3. Throughout the entire home, I added off-white sheer curtains with black wrought iron rods to create an immediate look of updated elegance.

4. I used bold red and black furniture as the home had light carpet, light floors, and lower-grade trim and finishes that lacked personality and interest. I brought in pillows, lamps, artwork, and

accessories in the same color scheme, and the home went from bland to bold, which made all the difference in the feel of the home.

5. The home had an awkwardly large space at the top of the stairs that lacked purpose, so I gave it purpose. I brought in a script wingback chair with an end table and lamp to create a cozy reading space for the buyer. I added colorful pillows and placed an afghan on the chair along with colorful accessories and a strategically placed book and coffee cup to emotionally connect the buyer and give the space the clear purpose it needed.

Testimony of Sale

This home had been on the market for 214 days with no offers, even after price reductions. It was put on the market after I staged it with the new real estate agent at a higher price than it was listed at before, and it was under contract in about a month!

Chapter 5

Staging Your Home: Smart Presentation Tactics

In this section, we will be learning about some challenging scenarios that come up in the world of staging and how to successfully address them.

Many times homeowners are faced with dilemmas in the listing process that are difficult to fix without expensive remodels or renovations, so we will be looking at some of these common issues and how to overcome them without having to break the bank!

A. Creating an Updated Look Through Staging

Creating an updated look is a great way to make your home look attractive while avoiding a costly remodel. When people come to view your home, they want to see your best home and don't want to feel like they are viewing an outdated, dusty, old one.

Even if your home is a little outdated, people appreciate character. And when something looks kempt, organized, and decorated, it's perceived value rises. Buyers need to feel glad they came to see your home, no matter what age it is!

In society today, house buyers are much busier, and people in general want things now. If someone perceives that your house is not well taken care of, this is what goes on in the back of their minds: "How long and what is it going to take for me to get this house back into shape?"

By spending a little bit of time and putting extra effort into creating an updated look, the time and money that would need to be taken by the buyer to update it will no longer prevent buyers from purchasing. Even if you are positive that a certain room needs a remodel but you do not have the time or money to do it, sprucing it up through staging and cleaning will make a huge difference.

DESIGN PRINCIPLE: Some repairs that you might want to think about that are not expensive for you to do are repainting old doors, repairing creaky stairs, and fixing leaky faucets. Repairing these issues will communicate great integrity in the eyes of the buyer if they do not need to be dealt with and will make your inspection process much easier!

The buyer might not be able to upgrade it right away, so at least they can see how to present it well now that you have made it look attractive as it is.

Here are six very practical tips that I have applied successfully over the years to achieve an updated look:

1. One of my favorites is by mixing your old items with new items.

   Think accessories. Mixing various items in the house with a few new things can help make an old house look stylish. Mixing saves money on staging, but make sure that it looks on purpose and put together. You can use the furniture in your house that still looks good while making some adjustments by adding some new accessories to them, such as throws or pillows.

   Remixing the items will also help you change your personal style of the room to a broader style that will be more appealing to the buyer.

2. Removing unnecessary knick-knacks and polishing and keeping surfaces clear give your listing a nice, neat look. This is especially effective in the kitchen and can help you make a small, cramped kitchen look spacious. One of the strategies I use to balance clear, spacious surfaces with the importance of décor is to create mini vignettes on black round placemats. On the placemats, I use strategic placement of color and textures, usually in threes, so that there is interest on the counters with the décor yet ample open countertop space between to keep it neat and organized looking.

3. My secret weapon for dated homes is what I call "the power of black and white." Adding black and white artwork is a great way to cut any drab colors or ugly textures in the room. This works great in rooms where there is old wallpaper, odd-colored tile or countertops that you might expect to have to replace, dated furniture, or obnoxious wall colors. I encourage you to try this strategy BEFORE suggesting expensive updates.

4. For lackluster rooms and homes with the bland off-white walls and off-white dated carpet, I like to use red, red, and more red! I consistently incorporate red in accessories like throws or pillows on the couch.

TIP: Hobby Lobby has an excellent section of pillow covers for $5 during the week they are 50% off (usually every other week), and they make a world of a difference!

5. Try to use some monochromatic flowers in beautiful vases (you can buy some inexpensive vases at Ross or Marshalls) throughout the house. Putting some nice fruit in a bowl on the coffee table also creates a nice updated look.

6. Another solution you can do to create an updated look is to go rustic with some of your older furniture, which has actually become a style rather than a fad. By doing a little faux finishing, you can make a lot of older things look on purpose by repurposing! You can also add some nice fixtures or handles with character that you can base the rest of the décor in the room on. Try a French theme, which will make some of your older furniture look a bit more modern. By enhancing the "old" look of furniture, you can create a style and character of your own that is attractive to buyers. Using this technique of mixing and adding a little pop of color with the décor will give you a nice, comfortable look in your house for buyers to walk through that will be pleasing and attractive to them!

B. Repainting, Repairs, and Renovations

Spending money on repairs can be a little costly at times but is often necessary, so saving money by staging instead of doing expensive renovations and repainting can be a huge relief for homeowners when preparing their house to be sold.

Repairs will usually come up in the inspection if you do not address them on the front end, so unless you are selling the property "as is," you probably need to invest in necessary repairs. Ensuring the house is in good repair is a more convincing sell for the buyer as it will help them have confidence that you have taken good care of the home, which helps support the value of the home.

Smart staging can often take the place of expensive renovations and repainting. When assessing the home, I make the decision in each room to either stage "toward" the home or "away" from the home. Staging toward the house is what you want to do when there is a beautiful element that you want to highlight or showcase with décor. Staging away from the house is what you want to do when there is a not-so-attractive element that needs to be minimized or distracted away from through the use of décor. This technique helps take away attention from any flaws in the house and guides people to bring their attention toward those things that are more pleasing to their eyes.

To paint or not to paint? Creating an on-purpose look is what we can do to avoid painting, no matter what the color. Take a look at the picture left with the eggplant

walls. Those walls were original, and we did not want to repaint them! So we styled the room to make the walls look on purpose. All it took was finding a comforter and some pillows to act as accents to pull everything together. Creating an on-purpose look in the realm of wall painting will save you a lot of time, energy, and money.

When you have a color in a room that is too bright or overdone, remember to use the power of black and white. It works every time!

C. Handling Design Blunders

Scenario 1: Unique Fireplace and Odd Flooring

1. The fireplace was dated, had a couple patterns of brick that did not match, and had a very old and worn black insert that looked dirty. The rest of the home was completely renovated, so it did not fit with the rest of the home.

2. The room was long and narrow, making it feel like a tunnel.

3. The floor was a very light color with a pattern, making the room feel like it was floating. The light color of the floor also created too much of a contrast with the fireplace, which further accentuated the dated fireplace.

Here are five things I did in staging to make the room work:

1. I brought in black and white artwork and chairs to neutralize and make the dated fireplace look fresh and classy.

2. Because the insert had a door that closed and covered the flames, I added a wrought iron candle holder with candles in the same tone of the brick color, providing the warmth and coziness flickering flames provide and buyers expect.

3. I added elegant pillows on the chairs in a similar tone to the fireplace to create a beautiful setting in front of the fireplace that helped the buyers see themselves relaxing and reading by the fireplace.

72

4. I added a natural woven rug on top of the flooring to break up the tile pattern and to create more softness and define the room.

5. I brought in a love seat that was scaled to the room and faced it toward the fireplace to create a comfortable conversation area and to cut the length of the room so that it no longer felt like a tunnel.

Each of these elements played a role in creating a successfully staged room, which spurred the house to sell after two showings in a matter of 14 days.

Scenario 2: High Light Fixtures and Small Dinette

The overall effect of this dinette should be cozy and romantic. Anytime you showcase a dinette, it is very important to use all the lighting you have as this gives the table an elegant finish.

First, we needed to bring in furniture and a tablecloth that would complement the space and color of the wall. Because there was such a small space to work with in this scenario, we wanted to create a feeling of ample room, which we did through the right size table and tablecloth. I carefully chose the material for the tablecloth and sewed the edges to create a custom look and feel for the room.

I added some tall, monochromatic flowers to give a visual connection between the tall fixtures and the table. Buyers' eyes need to take everything in at one time instead of letting their eyes move around. The color chosen for the flowers complemented the wall color as well as the table. For accessories, we added some elegant candle holders that enhanced the beauty of the table. We also added some black and white photos to complement the wall.

When faced with very bold or bright wall colors, monochromatic photos are great because they do not take away from or clash with the wall color and do not muddy the wall with more color that could potentially make it feel gaudy in the eyes of the buyer.

Some nice, soft sheers were also added to this room to give it a soft touch and to pull everything together. Through these steps, we were able to make the buyer feel welcomed, cozy, and luxurious in such a small space while tying everything together to create a designer look without the designer price.

Scenario 3: Small Entryway

The way to overcome a small entryway is by simply creating a settling place for people once they enter the home before transitioning into the next room. This is important as guests will enter the home and will need a place for their coats, shoes, and purses. One way to do this is by providing a landing path with a rug at the door and possibly a longer rug that connects the entryway to the room.

By doing this, the buyer will be able to enter the home and have a moment to comfortably adjust to the space before entering the rest of the home. You can provide a coat rack, a small entry table, or a wall-mounted coat hook next to the door. This helps you overcome the potential objection of not having an entryway or coat closet—they may not even notice! The key is to show the buyer how to work with the space in order to feel comfortable living in the home.

Scenario 4: Galley Kitchen

In a galley kitchen like this, it is important to create the feeling of spaciousness as the tendency can be to focus on the slimness of the space. The key to fixing this issue is to focus the buyer's eyes on beautiful things in the space and to strategically draw their eyes through the galley kitchen to the next room so that it feels like an extension of the space. In this example, the formal dining room was on the other side, so I created a dramatic look that captured the attention of the buyer. I also strategically created clusters of decor on the counter space—this balanced things and bounced the buyer's eyes from cluster to cluster to the end of the room and also created the illusion that there is a lot of space to utilize in this kitchen. Again, you are showing the buyer how to creatively live in the space they are in.

Scenario 5: Small Master Bedroom

Place your bedroom furniture in a way that makes the master bedroom look spacious and airy. You can use a full size bed rather than a queen, which helps the room look larger, and when possible, I put the bed at an angle to avoid the headboard going in front of a window.

Choose a nice, soft comforter on the bed with some pretty decorative pillows. Add nightstand tables or wooden TV trays on each side of the bed, or just one if that is all the space you have to work with. Placing a nice-sized lamp with accessories is a way to bring some elegance into the room. You can find nice pillows at Ross, Marshalls, or TJ Maxx at a great price.

Look for a nice throw for the end of the bed to create a soft, luxurious feeling that will make the buyer want to come home and relax in this room at night.

These tactics will help create the nice, elegant, intimate, and restful feeling we want the buyer to have when they walk into the master bedroom.

Scenario 6: Poor or Little Landscaping and a Plain Home Exterior

Staging also extends to the exterior parts of the home—after all, a buyer will make serious considerations of the exterior immediately upon driving up to the house. The more kempt, fresh, and attractive you can make the outside look, the better.

As far as the exterior of the house, it depends on how well the home has been maintained in considering if the owner wants to do a fresh coat of paint all around the house. A less expensive alternative is to make sure the exterior is clean by power washing the home and just painting the trim. Trim can brighten up the home and make it look like the whole house has received a fresh coat of paint!

The color and condition of the front door are key to getting your showing off on the right foot. Buyers want their homes to look nice, and one way to make the home visually attractive is to paint the door a nice color, such as a shade of red.

Your front door greets the buyer and communicates a lot about the home from the start. For example, if the front door is faded or outdated, the buyer will assume the rest of the home follows suit.

If you think you might need a new door, this would be a smart investment to make as it is a major part of the house that can make a big difference! Furthermore, a great place to stage is the porch of the home. If you have a porch, consider staging it with a patio table and chairs with a nice potted plant on top. This creates a comfortable, intimate scene outside the house for the buyer.

If you live in a well-traveled neighborhood, consider keeping the porch light on at night for buyers in the market who are passing by so they can admire what you've done! These small tips can enhance the exterior of your home and create a favorable impression on the buyer.

As far as the landscaping of the home, you can still achieve a nice earthy feel even if you don't have much to work with. The first thing you want to do is to start with a clean slate with a yard that is clean and cut. Next, we want to work with any opportunity areas in the landscape. If you see any eyesore barren areas, natural brown mulch is an affordable and excellent way to fill the space.

If you have a "no-scape" front yard, I encourage you to ensure you have some green plants or shrubs planted so it is not cold looking with all the rock and hard surfaces. An easy way to do this is to add big potted plants and flowers to the side of the doorway and in front of the house. This is a great way to spruce up your home for the buyer with minimal expense and to create a dramatic difference in the exterior of your listing.

Scenario 7: Too Much Space

If you have a room that serves no purpose in your house and you don't know what to do with it, imagine how the buyer would feel seeing an unstaged space and not understanding what to do with it either! This issue can be easily solved by staging the space and creating purpose for the room. If the room is near the kitchen, you can create a dining room or dinette. Either are very simple and affordable to put together. All you need is a table and chairs, table top décor, artwork, and some off-white sheer curtains with iron rods.

The table to the right is an oak table I grabbed at a garage sale for $25, and my son painted it black for me, which completely updated it for under $10. I purchased some elegant-looking chairs at American Furniture that were also affordable.

After the table is set up, scrunch a tablecloth (as mentioned earlier) to soften the room. Choose some big, beautiful, monochromatic flowers to act as the centerpiece, and add some plates to each setting with napkins and cutlery. Add a few candles for that nice, romantic touch, and voila! On the walls around the dinette, a few pictures can be added as well. Remember to bring as much light as possible into the room.

If the non-purposed room is in another area where a dining room would not make sense, try creating an office or conversation area. A conversation area can be put together with a sofa or loveseat, a couple of chairs, a rug, a lamp, a trunk for a coffee table, and a big photo or piece of artwork on the wall. A great place to go if you don't want to spend too much on this extra furniture is a thrift store or a garage sale. You can then dress up the furniture by purchasing a new, brightly colored afghan and decorative pillows and add to the trunk or coffee table a serving tray with some champagne glasses, soft ivy, and fake apples for a pleasing look. Use your imagination, and see what comes to life! Both of these examples will give the buyer a purpose for each and every single room in the house.

Chapter Summary

1. An updated look can easily be achieved by mixing the home-owner's current furniture and décor with some newer décor to create an updated look

2. Various ways we work through design blunders are through creative use of color, texture, and reasonably priced décor.

3. Demonstrating how to live in the house through savvy staging is one of the keys to overcoming design blunders in the home!

One of the real estate agents that I do a lot of home staging for called me to stage her personal home. What an honor! They had purchased a new home and were in the process of getting their current home ready for sale, so they were going through the house and deciding what updates and mainte-nance items should be completed.

Every home has fun design challenges, and this one had some unique items to address and work on. The homeowners had a challenge with their ceilings they inherited with the house that I had not run into before. The kitchen, dinette, and family room were one long, open space with a half wall to separate the dinette from the family room, and when I looked at the ceiling, they had popcorn texture on the ceiling in the kitchen and dinette area then a smooth knock down painted ceiling in the family room. The problem was it was all one long ceiling! So it looked very strange to see a transition in the middle of the expansive open ceiling.

They were trying to decide if they had to scrape the texture off and redo the kitchen and dinette, which is a very messy and labor-intensive job. They asked my opinion, and I suggested that they simply add a piece of molding along the transition line and paint it white to match the ceiling color. That way it provided a slight separation in the rooms that was very subtle, and it helped it look somewhat on purpose. They followed my advice, and no mention was made of the issue by the buyers.

Another unique challenge with this home was that the kitchen and part of the family room had a couple walls painted with a very bright blue; the paint color was a stark contrast to the rest of the walls, so it jumped out significantly as you walked into the home. I always do everything I can to avoid having

the homeowner have to paint walls, and this was a fun personal challenge for me to make it look like that wall color was done "on purpose" to complement the décor and design of the home. I tied the blue into the rest of the main level with accessories and pillows, and the home sold for asking price within three weeks of listing during the Christmas holiday season. The owners were thrilled with the results, and I was happy to be part of making that happen for them.

Testimony of Sale

The homeowners received a full-price offer within three weeks of listing the home during the Christmas holiday season. The sellers were thrilled and are happily moved into their new home. They know that home staging made all the difference for them in attracting a buyer so quickly at a solid price.

Chapter 6

Karen's Tips for Selling Your Home Fast

As a seller, you want your house sold as soon as possible, especially after finding another home. Supporting two properties can be expensive. If you are trying to sell your home in order to purchase another, this pressure can be daunting. However, with Karen's tips for selling your home faster, combined with the principles mentioned thus far in the book, you will be able to move forward with confidence!

A. How to Keep Your Home Staged

One of the best pieces of advice I can give you to sell your home faster after staging is to routinely clean your home and keep it staged! In order to keep it staged, you can follow just a few easy steps. They are as follows:

1. Take photos of each room after the whole house is staged, and reference your staging template during preparation time, before the buyer comes through the door.

2. Create a checklist of things to do based on the photos and template, and pull it out when you getting ready for a showing. It will make it easy to know what to do in each room.

3. In the process of keeping your home staged, if you have children, involve them in preparing for a showing by explaining to them their role and how they can pick out a few toys in their room to keep, box up the rest for the time being, or have a place for them to be neatly stowed away when buyers come to visit. This is a great way to involve children in the selling process, and they will feel so good when you get that offer knowing they contributed to the sale of the home!

FUN TIP: Show your family what their checklist looks like for when a buyer comes, and practice! You can do a "fire drill" and see how fast everyone can get the home ready to show as a fun activity.

If or when it gets difficult, just remember that these efforts, as well as any money you have spent on staging, are investments in order to get your home sold faster. Your buyer needs to see your staging efforts to win them over, so keep it staged!

Here is a sample checklist you might want to use to prepare your home before buyers come in the door:

Bathrooms

- Remove all personal products from sight, including the bath rug, and place them quickly in a clothes basket that gets put away in the closet for the showing.

- Quickly wipe down the counter and tub with Lysol wipes.

- Move the trash bin out of plain view.

- Make sure the room smells fresh. Keep some fresh linen spray handy if needed, and spritz your staging towels prior to the showing.

- Turn on the lights.

- Open any curtains, and set blinds to be perfectly perpendicular and all the way down to the window ledge.

- Light any candles.

Bedrooms

- Make the beds—use your photos for placement of the pillows on the bed.

- Make sure the room smells fresh—use linen spray if needed.

- Quickly dust the end tables—Lemon Pledge smells nice and clean.

- Stow away any personal objects from plain sight.

- Turn on the lamps.

- Turn on the ceiling light.

- Open the curtains, and set the blinds to be perfectly perpendicular and all the way down to the window ledge.

- Light any candles.

Kitchen

- Take out prepackaged chocolate chip cookie dough and put them in the oven, or take out some scented ornaments!

- Move the trash bin, dish soap, scrub buds, and refrigerator magnets out of plain sight.

- Wipe down counters with granite or multi-surface cleaner—make them shine!

- Make sure any food, pots and pans, and dirty dishes are put away.

- Put on some nice instrumental, either light classical or light jazz music.

- Turn on the lights, open any curtains, and light any candles.

Living Room

- Do a fast declutter of personal items.

- Plump pillows, and arrange them on your sofas and chairs as shown in your post-staging photos.

- Fold any afghans, and display as shown in your post-staging photos.

- Make sure the room smells nice—use linen spray if needed.

- Turn on the lights, open any curtains, and light any candles.

- At the end, if you have time, vacuum or sweep the floors, and clean any mirrors.

B. Final Remarks: Karen's Tips for Selling Your Home Fast

The number one strategy I would recommend to get buyers to fall in love with your house is to stage it according to the top three strengths that you find in your house.

If you have an elegant dining room as well as a beautiful dining table to match, make an amazing setting for the buyer to feast their eyes on! If you have a beautiful gazebo in the back yard with a hot tub, make sure it is well cleaned with a setting that includes towels and some children's gear or two wine glasses with roses in them next to a wine bottle.

If you have a beautiful master bedroom and bathroom, make sure they look absolutely breathtaking!

Staging the rest of the house according to how each room should feel to the buyer, again, is the best way to continue to decorate to sell your home faster. Each buyer, when they purchase a house, is going to do their best to make their new home feel and look the best way they can. If you can successfully do it for them, you are inspiring them with how to best decorate and live in yours!

Another key principle we have discussed is appealing to the buyer's emotions. We want to create an overall warm and inviting sense in the home, and we do this through various techniques, such as using soft textures and colors to create an intimate, comfortable feeling and creating pleasant scents throughout the home that are mild and as natural as possible. We also need to create as much light as we can in the home. Studies show that more light increases people's positive moods, and it highlights all of the staging you have put all your hard work into!

Use light music in the background to achieve a certain atmosphere of peace throughout the home. In addition, one of the classic techniques to creating a sentimental, attached feeling to the home is to bake a few cookies to appeal to that "Mom's homemade cookies" feeling that children experience when they are little… and I would still recommend this technique today!

Order, cleanliness, and a well-decorated home also create positive emotions for the buyer. This creates peace and a sense of care in the buyer's heart because they sense the home is well taken care of. This carries great value in how well your house is perceived by the buyer. People want to live in a well-kept home and will want to keep their new home looking that way.

If buyers see an unkempt home, this creates a bit of unrest and also a need for the buyer to see through the clutter, clean it up in their minds, and picture their things in a currently so-so home. We want buyers to pay what you are asking, and this is how we do it—by making the house look its BEST!

C. How to Create the Best MLS Listing on the Market!

Your MLS listing is one of the most important pieces of the puzzle when putting your house up for sale because this is how buyers will decide whether or not to come for a viewing. Buyers need to be

87

motivated to come to your house, and a common saying in the world of marketing is "The first thing you need to do is get buyers in the door!" In order to do this, you MUST first stage your home to its optimal look. Then look for a photographer with an eye for design. They will take the best photos of your house. This may seem expensive, but you can ask a friend or find someone on Craigslist for a very reasonable price that will be WORTH IT in the end! As far as deciding which photos to feature, choose the photos that feature the top three strengths of the house. Get the best angles and photos of these rooms, and feature them on the listing. Remember to leave out any parts of the home that are particularly unappealing. In addition, when taking photos of the bathroom, try not to let the toilet be a part of the picture. You want to focus on what's right with the home, not on what is wrong or unimportant. Of course, there are rooms that need to be featured, but if you have something that is discretionary and unappealing, choose not to use it. These tactics will be a key strategy in getting buyers in the door.

Just imagine a buyer scrolling through hours of photos to decide which house they are going to visit with the little time they have! You want to be one of those. These photos are the data they are using to rule out the houses they are not going to visit! So if you focus on the strengths of your house and take beautiful photos to feature in the MLS listing, you are going to get buyers in the door faster and therefore sell your house faster.

Chapter Summary

1. Keep your home staged in order to maximize the appeal of your home when buyers come through the door.

2. Appealing to the buyer's sense of smell, touch, and emotions will get them to fall in love with your house!

3. When displaying photos of your house on MLS, focus on the top three strengths of the house, and use your best photos. To have the best MLS listing on the market, hire a professional photographer to capture the best parts of the house.

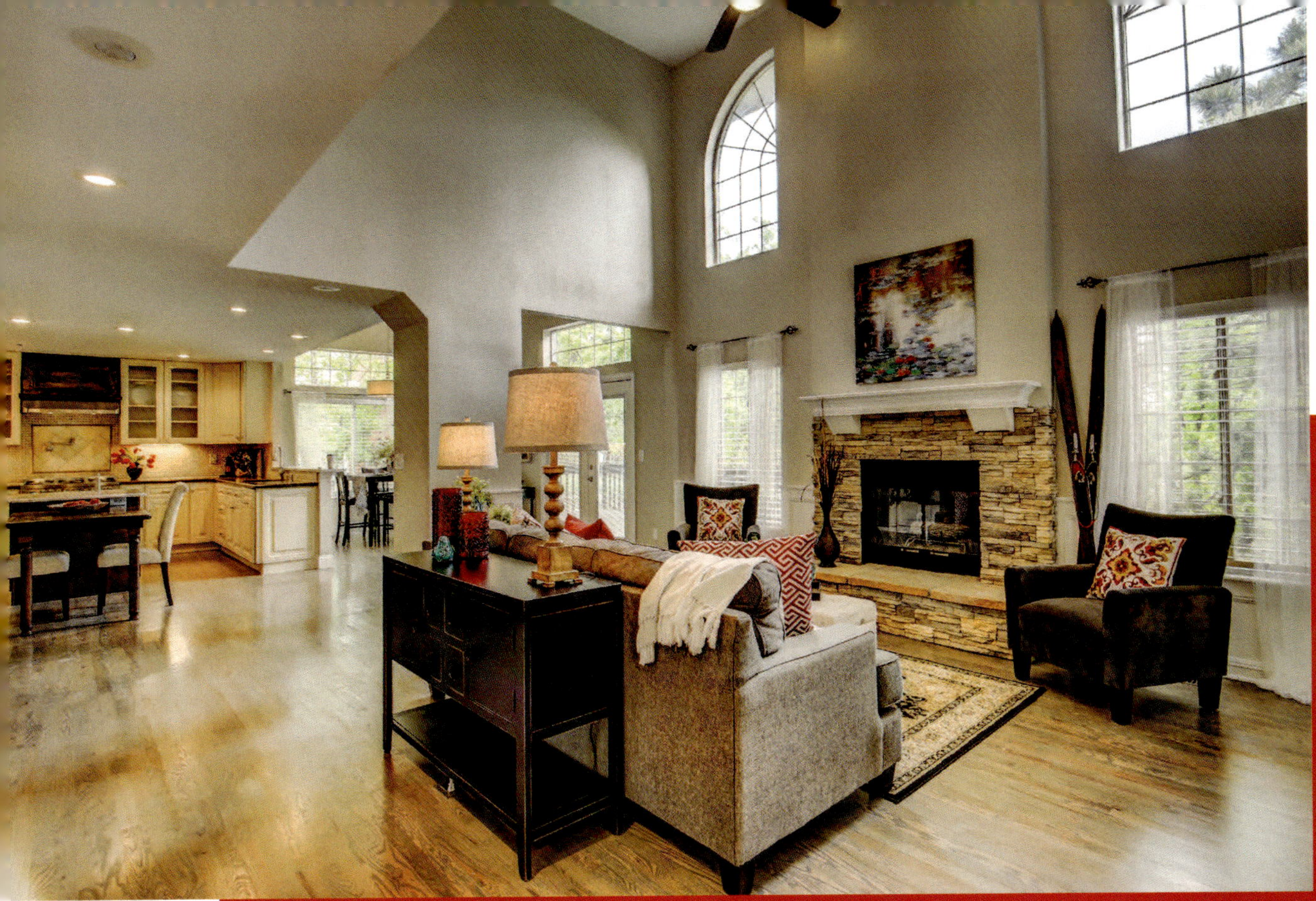

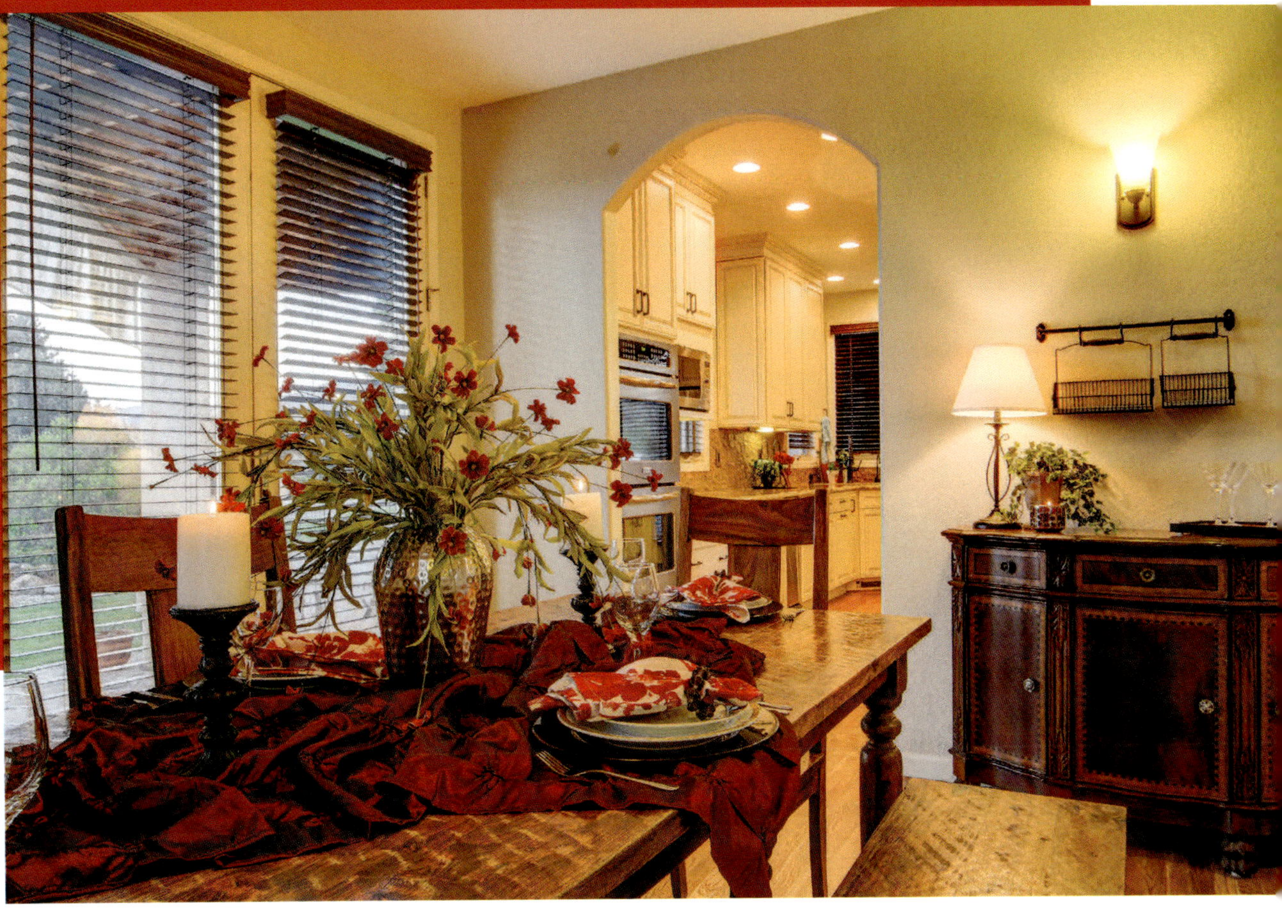

Chapter 7

A Redesign Case Study: SOLD to the First Buyers Through the Door After It Was Staged

After sitting dormant on the market for 124 days, the agent of this listing called me in to take a look at the house. I was hired, and after a few days, the staging was complete. We uploaded photos on MLS and got two immediate showings.

The first buyers through the door after it was staged purchased the home! Why was staging so effective for this home?

91

I believe it is because this beautiful home needed just a few things to give the potential buyer a reason to **buy the home** instead of a reason **not to buy the home**. What do I mean by that?

When inquiring with the listing agent and the homeowner about the feedback provided during the four months it had been on the market, the reasons potential buyers

gave when letting them know they were not interested in the home ranged from the house being too big, to the kitchen being outdated, to not liking the layout of the master bathroom, etc.

As I walked through the home, none of these reasons were show stoppers, so it was obvious to me they had to come up with something because there was nothing about the home that captured their heart and emotions. Boom! I had just located the strategy for staging the home.

I will be documenting each room in the home and explaining the design plan I put together for each room. I will share with you my design plans for one of the rooms to give you an idea of how I connected the potential buyer to the home.

The main picture in this chapter is the "after" of the office at the front of the home. The seller has beautiful artwork, and I just love the mixture of old and new with the furniture and artwork, but we were missing some things that I easily corrected through home staging.

In my experience as a home stager, when I am called in to help get a listing sold that is already priced right and in overall good shape but just not selling, I look for two things:

1. What is the potential buyer seeing in the first 7–10 seconds? Is it giving them something to LOVE during that time so that they are emotionally connecting right away? If we do not grab them in that initial time frame, the opportunity to connect with them is gone.

2. Are there rooms where the function is not clear? If the buyer cannot see themselves in the home and understand the purpose for each room, it leaves them with questions about how to live in the home that need to be answered in their house hunting process.

Both of the above were occurring with potential buyers of this home, and I knew just how to get it corrected, starting with the office!

1. I started "shopping" in the home to fill voids in the office and other rooms. The seller had beautiful pieces in the butler's pantry cupboards that I pulled from and repurposed to make the office feel warm and purposeful.

2. I displayed crystal pieces on the end table and on hutch shelves, and I brought in a substantial artificial ivy to add softness and interest to accent the beautiful pieces. The "before" picture below has items on the shelves, but when I arrived, all those items had been removed. Also, the curtains had already been removed, which helped to bring light into the room.

3. As you can see below, there was an upholstered dated rocking chair in the corner but no desk, which is the main staple to a home office. I brought the rocker out to the garage, and I brought in a small desk and pulled an extra side chair from the dining room to make the front office functional and beautiful.

4. I added a generous floral piece and brought in books from the seller's reading collection that have colors in the cover that contributed to the overall theme and color palette of the room.

5. I placed the desk at an angle looking out to engage the potential buyers from the entrance.

Think of it as creating a display for your audience; each room incorporates elements that "wink" to your potential buyer.

The result was a beautiful office that contributed to the overall look and feel of the home while communicating functionality and beauty.

TIP: I like placing old books throughout the houses I stage, and when possible, I prefer to use large picture books of area attractions and landscapes, which add a very nice touch.

Before

95

As you walk in the home, the formal dining room is the first room on the right. It is a beautiful room, but there were a few things that needed to be adjusted for the room to "feel" right as you walked in, and table décor needed to be added to help potential buyers envision having holidays and special occasions in the room with friends and family.

Here is what I did to bring out the best in the dining room:

1. The table was set at an angle so that it would fit in the room, but it made the room look small, and the room did not feel like it was in order. We removed one of the leaves so that the table would easily fit on the area rug and straightened the table back out to work the angles of the room, which made the room much more functional.

2. I brought in table décor to complement the room, including a tall, floral, red-textured square tablecloth with a sheen that I scrunched to create elegance and softness. I added chargers, plates, silverware, and crystal to show off the beauty of the home.

3. I moved a small accent table from the corner to against the wall and added a small lamp, greenery, and a small picture on an easel to create interest and complement the other décor in the room.

96

Before

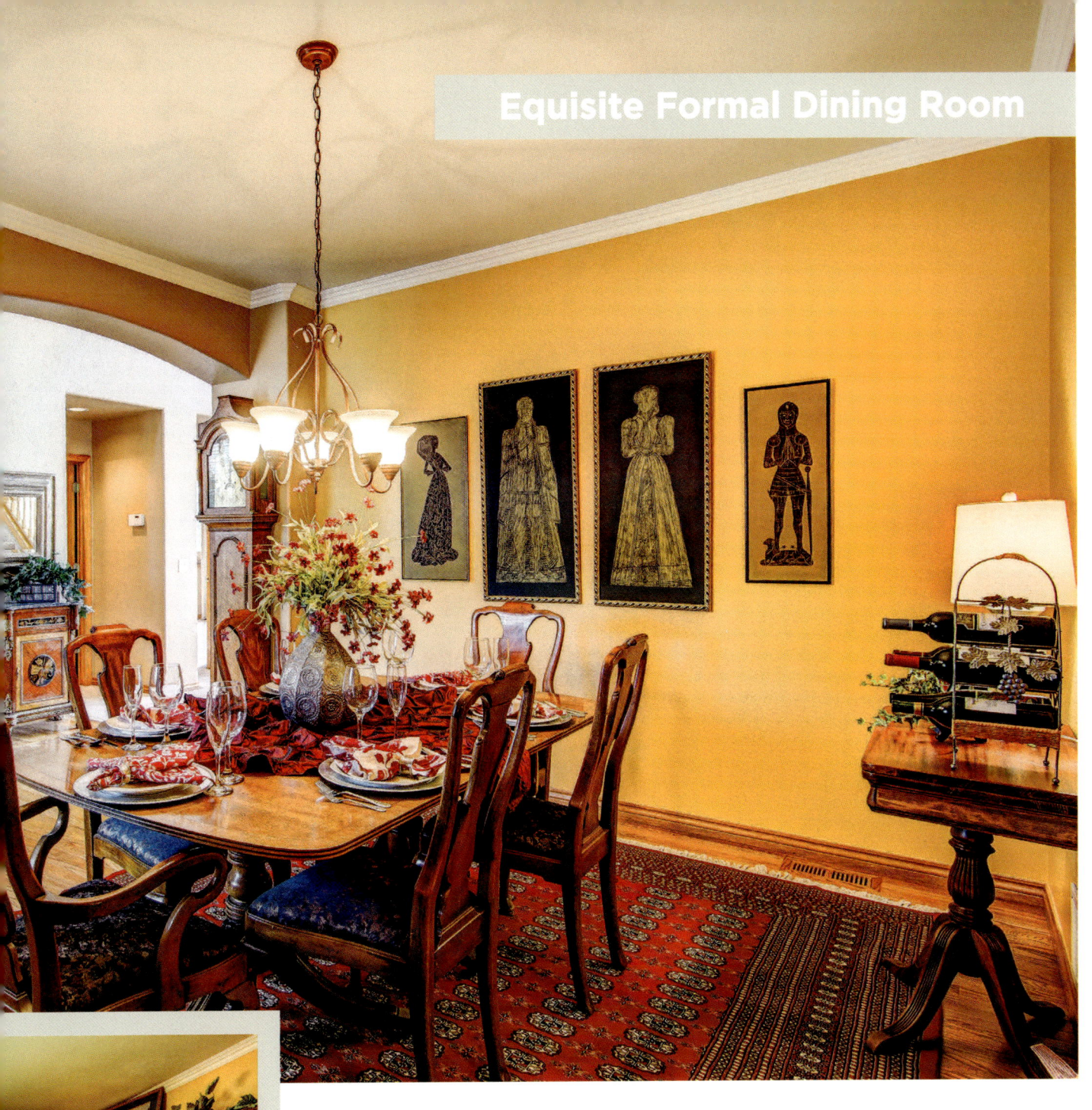

4. I removed pictures that did not reflect the elegance and style of the room and replaced them with simple artwork, adjusting the height to eye level from too high. (This is a common issue I see in homes and is easy to fix.)

5. I staged a few pieces of crystal in the hutch, and the room was all staged and ready to "wow" the buyers as they stepped into the home.

97

As you enter the home, straight ahead is the formal living room. Here is the explanation of the five things I did in the formal living room to help this sell to the first buyer!

1. The sofa and furniture in the room were older and somewhat out of date, particularly the sofa and wingback chair. Using updated pillows that connected the blue wingback chair to the sofa, red pillows to give the room some "pop," and script pillows to give it an updated look with the popular Paris theme, I was able to give the furniture an instant facelift with minimal investment.

2. The baby grand piano was beautiful, but it needed some softness and purpose brought to it so that it felt warmer and less formal. I brought out some sheet music to place on the piano so that it looked inviting and purposeful, pulled a vase from across the room and placed it next to the piano on the floor, and added some natural foliage to bring some softness to the formality.

3. The blue wingback chair was dated, but I added a throw and updated pillow to add interest and placed an open book on the chair so that the buyers could imagine themselves relaxing in front of the fireplace after a long day's work.

TIP: If you have outdated colors in a room on the walls or with a piece of furniture, use black and white artwork or accessorize—it cuts the outdated color and gives an instantly elegant and updated look to any room.

Before

99

4. Every room needs some pop of warm color with red or orange, and in this case, I added some soft ivy to the end table, which was greatly needed with all the hard finishes, and then added an orange-red ceramic bird, the red pillows, and some beautiful natural-looking apples in a white container that was previously placed on the kitchen dinette table. The red accessories made such a difference in the look of this room; it helped it become warm and inviting instead of cool and stale.

5. To accessorize the fireplace and create that picture-perfect view of the living room in the first seven seconds, I moved a vase with willows in it from the formal dining room and placed in on the hearth of the fireplace. With that vase, along with the work I did that was listed above, I could begin to draw the buyer's attention to the beautiful fireplace and formal living space I had created, in the first seven seconds of entering the home.

6. I also pulled the items that were on the shelf above the fireplace together, added a soft plan, and pulled them together in an arrangement that was pleasing to the eye and connected so that the buyer's eye could take it all in together, which is really important when creating those perfect spaces to please our "audience," which is the potential buyer.

This home had a beautiful master bedroom, and the homeowner's furniture was really nice, but it was a little too obvious that it was a bachelor pad. It needed some nice, soft touches to help it feel like a romantic retreat. I used most everything the homeowner already had in place and added just a few touches.

Here is what I did:

1. My goal was to lighten things up and create a relaxed feeling in this room. As you can see, the bedding is beautiful, but it needed a little color. So I added a few spring green pillows along with a navy and off-white patterned accent pillow to tie everything together.

2. For this room, I wanted to create interest and send the right message to the buyer. At first glance, the end tables lacked accents and softness, so I added a wooden "LOVE" sign to the larger end table, along with some greenery. Then, to add a touch of personality, I added a simple ceramic bird to the smaller end table.

3. I continued with the spring color accents in the bedroom by adding a black vase of green apple blossoms to the side of the

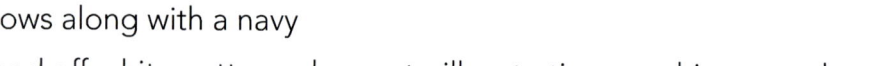

bed and to freshen up the look of the dresser.

4. The first view of the master bedroom was actually a wall (not shown in this photo), so I hung a picture to introduce the spring green color used throughout the room and to add an immediate feminine touch to it. Women have a LOT of influence on house purchase decisions, so I did this knowing the master bedroom and bathroom could either make or break the sale—which, in this case, made the sale in two days.

5. In order to create a nice tie between the leather chair and the bed, I added a spring green afghan with a matching accent pillow.

6. To immediately greet potential buyers and make the master bedroom look like a romantic getaway, I added a tray with greenery, red apples, and champagne glasses, which was placed at an angle on top of the cedar chest at the foot of the bed. This tray with décor communicates relaxation and vacation, which is exactly what we want to plant in the mind of the buyer upon entering the room.

Before

103

Master Bathroom Hideaway

104

To give you some background information, a common comment on this home prior to the seller considering staging was that potential buyers did not like the actual layout of the master bathroom. As I studied the bathroom and considered the comments, it became clear to me that the layout was probably not the real issue. Rather, the bathroom looked less than luxurious for this price of home, and it needed to be given a designer look.

One of the most effective ways to create an elegant look in master bathrooms is to use black and white, as it adds drama, and to bring in deep green towels to add some color.

Before

105

Here is what I did to give the master bathroom an easy makeover:

1. The homeowner had many pictures tucked away in closets, which were not being used, and I located some black and white drawings of an English countryside that worked perfectly for the open walls of the bathroom. I placed one of them in a visible location from the doorway to ensure potential buyers would get a full view of the staging at first glance of the master bathroom.

2. I placed deep green bath towels on the towel bars and folded one of them carefully over the tub with a high-quality, fragrant bar of soap so that buyers could envision themselves relaxing in the tub.

3. To the vanity on the left, I added white florals in a silver vase angled toward the doorway for a soft and romantic look. To add some interest and additional fragrance, I added decorative potpourri in the same green and white colors.

4. On the second vanity, I placed an old, silver, mirrored tray that I found at a flea market, which worked beautifully for this room. The homeowner had beautiful crystal champagne glasses that I placed on the tray along with a small bundle of white roses to add to our romantic look.

5. Finally, behind the tray, at an angle, I placed chunky black candle holders with deep green candles to complete the makeover of the bathroom.

Before

The feedback received on this house while on the market for the 124 days often included that the kitchen was outdated. When I looked at the kitchen, it did not seem to be particularly outdated however; rather, there was nothing to "love" about it.

So my job was to figure out how to stage it to look more expensive and interesting to the buyer. Here is what I did with the kitchen:

1. The eating area in the kitchen was nice with its updated light fixture, but it needed a more dramatic feel when looking into the kitchen from the formal living room. A floral arrangement would give it some color and texture, so I added a black vase with spring green-colored florals, which gave it the look it needed!

2. For the workspace in the corner of the kitchen, I wanted to ensure it was functional in order to show off the value of the built-in desk. The kitchen had a very large plate that was in the corner by the wall, which overpowered the space. I removed the large plate and replaced it with a cozy lamp, ivy, and accessories to show off the upgraded desk.

3. The kitchen had a beautiful hardwood floor, but the home-owner had two rugs displayed that were distracting and felt out of place. In order to bring balance to the room, I removed the small rug in front of the kitchen sink and replaced it with the longer rug, which is really elegant. This seems like a subtle change, but it made a big difference in the look and feel of the kitchen for the buyer.

4. The counters were a quality solid surface, but the gray looked cold and drab with no accessories, and despite brand new stainless steel appliances, it still looked like an outdated, lower-quality kitchen. I used round black placemats to provide the base for accessories to be neatly placed on the kitchen counters and added black and white napkins in wine glasses, greenery, a small ornate framed painting that I brought from another room in the house and hung between the counter and cupboard, and a tray with the homeowner's coffee mugs, which always helps plant a seed of family gatherings in the family kitchen.

112

Before

The powder room is a small space with a big impact. Why? This bathroom is used by guests, and when decorated nicely, it communicates hospitality.

Here are a few things I did in the powder room that made it look almost like a totally different room!

1. I added a small black vase with lily-of-the-valley florals to provide an immediate "wow" to potential buyers as they peeked into this small bathroom.

2. Above the toilet, I used one of my signature items—a canvas with black and white script material stretched over it. You certainly know by now that black and white is one of my favorite ways to bring out the best in a bathroom!

3. In order to tie the bright green, black, and white colors together in the powder room, I used some bright spring green towels. I draped one of them over the towel bar, and the other I folded with a black ribbon to provide a very bold look.

4. One of the easiest things you can do to make an above-the-toilet storage cupboard look clean and elegant is to add several inexpensive white candles in glass across the shelf. Always use an odd number, either five or seven.

TIP: You can purchase these for just a few dollars a dozen, and they also look great for photos in a shower or tub area when lit.

Before

This house had a great walkout lower level, but it was a "man cave," as it looked a little drab and uninteresting, and it needed some color.

I left most everything in place and simply added a few details to make the room more inviting.

1. The tan couch was quite worn and old, so I needed to draw attention away from the actual piece of furniture. What better way to do this than adding some decorative pillows! I added some larger pillows, not too feminine, in red, black, and white. Red always adds warmth to a room, which was much needed here.

2. To the coffee table, I added some red florals and placed two unique candle-holders on top, which were relocated from another part of the room. I added red candles inside the holders and placed some nice picture books on top as a finishing touch.

3. I also laid an afghan over the back side of the couch. What you cannot see is that it covered a very worn-out part of the sofa, so it was strategically placed.

TIP: I like placing old books throughout the houses I stage, and when possible, I prefer to use large picture books of area attractions and landscape, which add a very nice touch.

Chapter 8

Before & After Photos: Vacant & Occupied Homes

In this next section, you will be able to see different scenarios of staging in a vacant home. Before and after photos will be shown in order to understand the process we went through to get from the unstaged home to a staged home! From these examples, you will be able to gather enough insight and information to make an incredible and meaningful transformation to your own home!

Before

Vacant Home Photos

A vacant home is an empty house and requires a full staging effort! This will include adding furniture, décor, and other accessories, such as flowers, candles, and tablecloths to win the heart of the buyer. From these photos of fully staged vacant homes, you will be able to understand how to add various items to a vacant home in order to create a welcoming and elegant style to attract buyers and make your home sell faster!

119

Eggplant Dream

Before

My Golden Living Room

Before

122

Pop of Pink Banquet

Before

French Quarters

Before

126

Mauvelous Dinette

Before

Home Sweet Cottage

Before

Simply Grand Fireplace

Before

Kissable Creations

Before

No Remodel Bathroom

Before

137

138

Dark Chocolate Master Bathroom

Before

139

Paris Powder Room

Before

140

Dainty Dinette

Before

141

Before

142

143

Classy Kitchen

Before

144

Warm Spring Bedroom

Before

Before

A Fine Time Living Room

Step 1

Before

150

Step 2

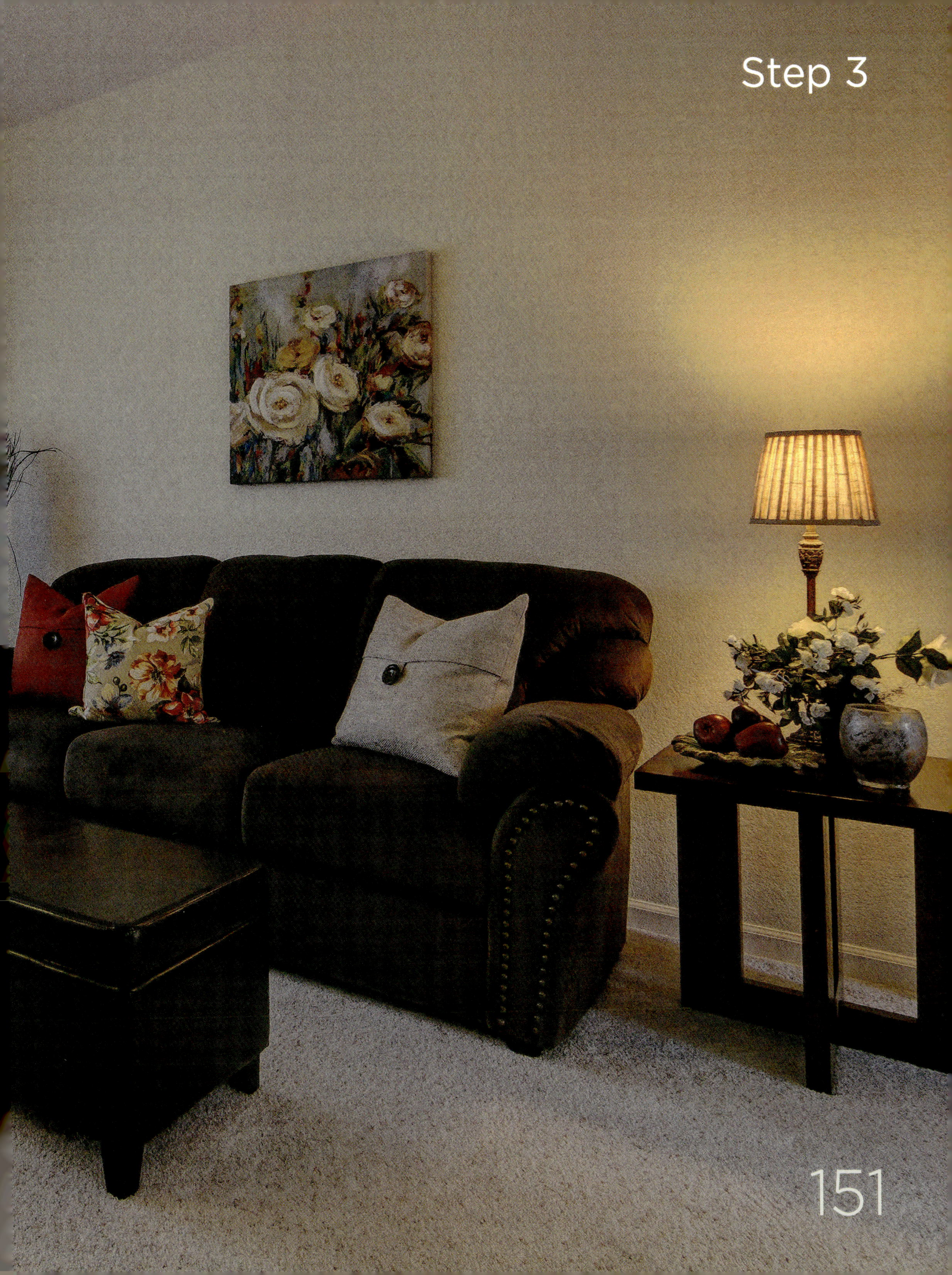
Step 3

Step 2

Step 3

Step 1

Before

orner

153

Before

155

Young n' Fun Powder Room

Before

Green Forest Powder

Before

157

Kitchen With Character

Step 1

Before

Step 3

Step 2

159

Before

161

Gold-Kissed Hideaway

Ivy Wild Kitchen

Before

164

Delicate Red Powder Room

Before

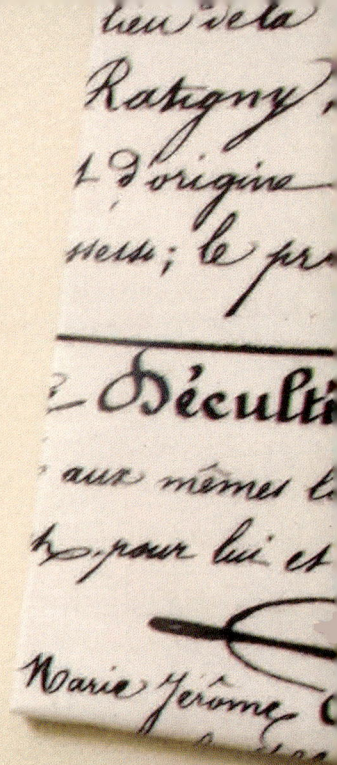

167

168

Before

170

Floral Bath

Before

English Study

Before

Occupied Home Photos

In this section, you will be able to see original "redesigns" from an occupied home. The great advantage about occupied staging is that you can use your own personal furniture to save money on staging costs. The art of redesigning a home is enhancing the current furniture and décor in order to create an appealing style that will attract the eyes of the buyer. Take a look at the following photos, and be inspired to create a brand new look in your house!

Leisure Living Room

Before

Lovely Living

Before

Before

178

Rustic Relaxation

Before

181

Before

182

183

Escape to Italy

Before

184

Queen's Palisade

Before

187

Pottery Bath

Before

A Feminine Touch

Before

Delightful Master Suite

Before

192

193

194

195

Calm Flower Shower

198

Youthful Gaze Kitchen

Before

200

202

Rose Bath

Before

203

Sweet Apricottage

Before

204

A Cabiner's Dream

Soft Lodge Haven

Before

Bonus: How Not to Break the Bank

Staging the house does not have to be a huge expense. While you may have seen expensive décor for houses online or on TV, you can easily access such pieces inexpensively from stores that sell these products at affordable prices.

A. My Top-Choice Stores to Buy Inexpensive Décor

There are a great number of stores that sell house décor items at very affordable prices. One of my favorite places to buy furniture when I need it is American Furniture.

I find great ottomans as well as old books that I place in my houses.

Ross is a "go to" for me for many things, and the most common items I purchase there are decorative pillows, bedding sets, artwork, and curtain rods.

Hobby Lobby has great decorating items. I have purchased decorative bowls, pillow covers, monochromatic flowers, and other items for less than $20! They have sales every other week for 50% off and an ongoing 40%

of one regular-priced item coupon, so with a little planning, you can usually get a good deal!

Walmart is another one of my favorite stores to visit. When I need an item on the fly or at night, when all the other stores are closed, it is a great option! They have everything you need at extremely fair prices. You can get colored candles, bathroom towels, curtain rods, and curtain sheers to give a room just the right touch for under $10, every day of the week. I have been known to go to Walmart at 4 a.m. to get the finishing touches on a home I am staging! I have worked through many nights to get things just right for my clients by the date they needed it to go on the market.

At Walmart, I also frequently purchase Christmas wreaths, black circle mats, and air mattresses to go on bedframes to stage the master bedroom. Some of these items cost so little, and you can easily use them to change the style of your own house!

Target also has some great deals on tablecloths, rich green towels for the bathroom, and wall hooks for the entryway. This is a great place to shop for nice, elegant accessories to enhance the look of your house.

For higher-end items, I go to Home Goods or Marshalls and may only pick out one or two items but will build the look of the room around those pieces.

You can also get amazing deals online at stores such as Amazon or eBay. Do a quick search for the item you need, and you can buy inexpensive items and have them delivered to your door! These are great ways to s ave money on staging.

Each of these stores have different items that will make your house look pleasing to the buyer at affordable prices. You can save money whether you are doing vacant house staging or occupied home staging!

B. DIY Designer Décor

There are some very simple things you can do to achieve a designer look for your house! I do it all the time and actually sew or make a significant number of my core pieces.

There are many items that you can pick out in stores that are beautiful in themselves, and when added to the house, they create a designer look that is attractive to buyers. There are also many items you can make to bring a unique designer look to your listings without the designer prices!

I go to the dollar store or to Walmart, purchase clear glass vases, and paint them to provide a designer look. This particular vase I used next to the apples is an inexpensive glass vase with black watercolor paint. I would get a good amount of paint and just let it drip down the vase.

Sheer curtains also create a simple and beautiful designer look. Something so sheer next to pillows that have bold and beautiful colors levels out the look and makes the room look very classy in the eyes of the buyer. I purchase inexpensive sheer curtains from Ikea or

213

Walmart and hang them on black wrought iron rods to create an airy look and feel that can change the look and feel of a room in minutes!

For the dinette, you can also create your own table by purchasing one at a garage sale or a thrift store. Sand the table and repaint it, and then sand it again in order to create a nice, rustic look. I have painted oak tables black, and it looks awesome. Add some fabric chairs for a dramatic contrast, and you have just remodeled your dinette for a minimum investment.

I find great tablecloth or runner fabric, pick out coordinating napkin fabric to sew custom table décor, and have the foundation for an amazing, beautiful table! All you need is an eye for design and a sewing machine, and you can do wonders!

Hobby Lobby is a great place to find items that create a designer look and feel for your home. For example, I have an affinity for creating unique, designer serving trays. You can find one of theses in every home that I stage!

You can make these inexpensively by purchasing a picture frame, scrapbook paper, framing matte paper, and drawer pulls, which are attached to the ends of the picture frame to become handles for the tray. Here is how you make these trays:

1. Purchase an 8 ½ by 11 or 9 by 12 frame with substantial depth so that you can drill holes and screw in the handles.

2. Choose the scrapbook paper you want to use, and cut it to the size of the frame.

3. Place the paper in the frame so that it shows through the glass, and glue and staple gun framing matte cardboard to the bottom for a finished look.

4. Screw holes in the sides of the frame, and screw in the handles on each side.

This is a fantastic item to use in the living room or in a bedroom to create a nice bed and breakfast look!

C. Creating a Christmas Look

I am a big fan of Christmas decorating because it brings back pleasant family memories for everyone. An excellent way to add flair to your home staging, a little bit of Christmas décor helps the buyer visualize themselves spending Christmas with their family inside the home. Sometimes people think Christmas decorating can be expensive, but it doesn't need to be. Purchasing a few poinsettias at the grocery store and placing them around the house can make a big difference. In addition, as you can see in several of these Christmas photos, you can purchase items in bulk, like burlap ribbon and berries, and use them throughout the house. I used berries and burlap ribbon for my bathroom towels, front door wreath, and pillows. Another easy idea is wrapping some empty presents and placing them throughout the house. A few simple things can make your house feel like a home and will go a long way in the eyes of the buyer.

D. Chalkboard Coaster Feature – For Under $2

What a great conversation piece and ice-breaker for any event!

1. Go to the dollar store and buy a candle plate for a dollar.

2. Paint your coaster with chalkboard paint.

3. Hand these out to your guests to write some fun messages!

4. What's your message?

Read Karen's blog and subscribe for updates and information at **KarenConrad.net**!

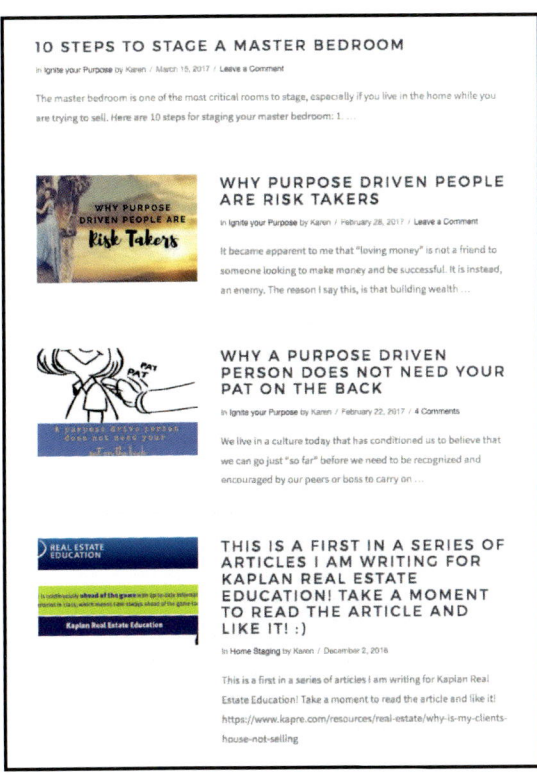

Subscribe for your free e-book!
Bargain Buys

KarenConrad.net

Karen is on Facebook, Twitter, LinkedIn and Youtube!

10 Table Inspirations for Every Season

When staging a home, I have hundreds of combinations that I use for dining tables. Here are the components I use to make the table look custom and tie completely into the décor of the home. It's much easier than you think!

1. I pick out material to make a runner or a square tablecloth that serves for the foundation of the design.

2. Choose a tall vase and monochromatic florals to complement and add beauty and texture to the table. Oversize florals work great for a dramatic touch.

3. Purchase material that complements the other elements, and sew napkins for an instant designer impact!

4. Make or purchase napkin rings that go with the style of the table. Use chargers in various colors to add a finished look to your table, and it also serves a functional purpose of protecting your table from your china. Use your favorite china; I often use white or off-white so that I can put any design or color with it. I often buy my plates at Marshalls, Home Goods, or Ross as you can pick up high-quality dinnerware at these stores at a great price.

5. Choose your wine glasses or goblets. I use dollar store glassware—it's durable and available in several colors and styles.

6. Add candle elements to the table, either on a candle holder or using small votives to add a romantic feel to your dining room setting.

7. At holiday time, I bring in the natural elements that I use on artificial trees, like eucalyptus, baby's breath, and red berries, and integrate that into the table to tie the entire holiday look and theme together.

221

Chapter 10

Now It's Your Turn!

Now that you have seen a practical case study and some additional before and after staging examples, it is time to look at a home staging recipe that you can follow on your own! The following pages are a guide to show you how to stage each room of the house. In this guide, I have provided a checklist of items to use for each room along with how to keep track of where you will be getting these items from (whether you have the item on hand or need to purchase it). In addition, I have provided a step-by-step process on how to stage each room. I would love to hear about the success of your efforts, so during your home staging journey, stop by and visit KarenConradHome. com and contact me to tell me all about it!

Living Room

Items	Have Item	Purchase Item
Couch		
Substantial side chairs		
1 or 2 end tables		
Coffee table or large bench/trunk or 2 basket trunks		
7 pillows (5 for couch, 1 for each chair)		
1-3 pictures or series of artwork		
2 candleholders for fireplace, 1-3 additional for end table and coffee table		
3-5 ivy or other greenery		
2-3 planters for plants		
Floral with vase for end table or coffee table		
Coffee table tray		
Afghan		
3-5 hardcover books for accents and height help		
2 lamps		
Small or large apples, in red or green		
1-2 medium candle holders with candles in metal or mercury for end table or coffee table		
Small decorative wood or metal sign with uplifting message (e.g., Bless This Home, etc.)		
2 wine or champagne glasses		
1 or 2 coffee cups		
Ceramic bird or other items in red, orange or bright green		
Tall vase with dried weeds for fireplace hearth, if appropriate		

1 Place the couch in the room first; it is often placed in front of the fireplace at the same angle and usually "floats" in the room, not usually against a wall—unless it is a smaller living room where conversation can take place in the space easily.

2 Once the couch is placed, put the two chairs either at a right angle to the couch or, in some cases, at a 45-degree angle on each side of the fireplace. The room will dictate which works better; generally, in a tight space, you will use the chairs at the angle of the fireplace.

3 In a living room with no fireplace, you will want to arrange the furniture based on a window or the entrance of the room. For example, if the room is a separate space (not an open floor plan), I often will have the couch floating, facing the two chairs, with the coffee table in between. This keeps the room "open" and inviting while being able to "wow" the buyer upon entrance of the room with color and style with the furniture.

4 Artwork over the fireplace should be no more than six inches off the mantle so that the artwork and the fireplace are viewed as one, not separate.

5 For the mantle, depending on the size of the fireplace, I will usually place two candle holders on one side of the artwork, with a book to add height and ivy to fill in the space and to add texture. Then, on the other side of the artwork, either leave empty or you can have a single candleholder that goes with the other two candleholders tucked in front of the frame—or you could have a lantern with additional accessories to provide a nice balance.

226

6 Place the end tables between the chairs if they are side by side or beside the couch on each side so that they are still somewhat close to the chairs placed at a right angle and the furniture is all connected.

7 Place a lamp on each end table; then do a group of two or three on the table next to the lamp to give it a polished look. (See pictures of examples of groups that work well on an end table.)

8 On the coffee table or trunks, I usually place a tray at an angle then place books for height and color along with an ivy or florals, candle holders, apples, wine glasses, or coffee mugs. Take into consideration the other elements you have used in the room, and try to have a nice variety. One tip is to use the rounded plants from Ikea as a nice mix of textures and color so they are not all ivy or exactly alike.

9 Use five pillows for the couch, three or four for the loveseat, plus an afghan. The pillows are usually two sets of pillows—one set in warm colors, one set in cold colors—then an accent pillow to add color and splash. I often use just one set the same then mix and match with the additional three. I use a set of matching pillows most often on the accent chairs, but you may also use an afghan on one chair and a pillow on the other for interest.

227

Kitchen

Items	Have Item	Purchase Item
Hand towels		
2 wine glasses + napkins		
Black mats		
Books		
Ivy		
Glasses or bowls with fruit to put inside		
Little sign with a message		
Small hanging picture		

1. Focus on the counters

   a. Clear the counter of any items. As a general rule, we use black mats and place them strategically on the counters in any "bare areas." If you have a corner, place one there, and add a lamp or puck light if there are not under-the-cabinet lights installed. Put clusters of three objects on top of the mats.

   b. Mix color, texture, and height with the objects that are placed on these mats. For example, you can use ivy around each of the items and put a plant on a book or two. Put two wine glasses with napkins inside them, or put out a little sign with a message.

   c. The main strategy is to make it look spacious, not cluttered, and accentuate the features in the kitchen.

Focus on hand towels

   a. These should be colorful. You can place the hand towels on the counter next to the sink, or you can put them on the stove handles. If towels are placed next to the sink, position them at an angle.

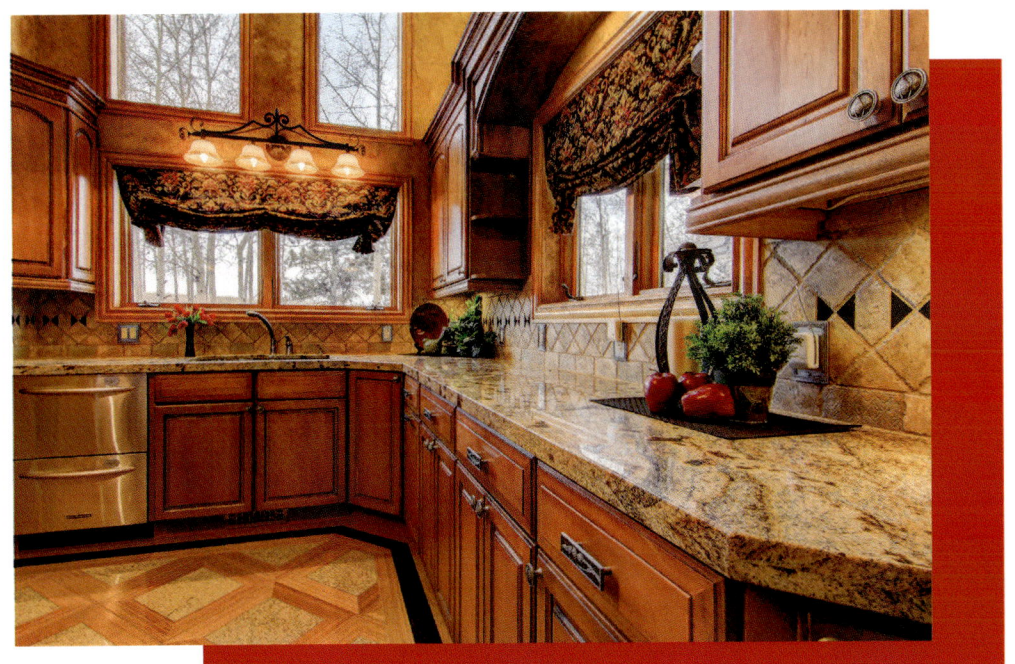

229

3 Focus on hanging a small picture

     a. You can hang it on the wall or between the counter and the cabinets.

4 Focus on the kitchen window

     a. If there is a window in the kitchen, consider hanging a scarf over the window. Generally, I will go with an off-white or white sheer fabric for the scarf. If you can sew, it is really easy! Just get about three yards of sheer material (of course, it will vary depending on the size of the window), cut the ends at an angle, and simply hem the two ends. The selvage takes care of the parallel sides of the fabric, so no sewing is needed for the long edges of the fabric. You can either use a rod and drape the fabric over it with loops hanging down about 12 inches or you can purchase tie backs for smaller windows and tie a loose knot on the ends with a nice dip over the window.

5 Focus on extra features

    a. If the kitchen has a decorated storage space in the walls or cabinets, fill the spaces, but you don't have to fill every box or space provided.

    b. If there is a bar looking into the kitchen, put some sort of a tray, and center it with three wine glasses to draw guests into the kitchen.

Powder Room

Items	Have Item	Purchase Item
4 hand towels		
Candle(s)		
Sheer shower curtain		
Tall floral and vase		

1 Focus on choosing your colors

    a. General rule: You want to be bold and dramatic with your colors. For bold-colored walls, use black and white pictures. For neutral-colored walls, match the pictures to complement the florals.

2 Focus on the sink

    a. This is where your floral goes. Choose one that is tall and large and that covers a little bit of the mirror. NOTE: Select flowers that look natural. Hobby Lobby is a great place to find these. If you have a narrow sink but your vase fits, do not worry about practicality—oversize is what catches attention.

    b. NOTE: We are assuming your sink has a mirror. If it doesn't, create one. Hang a drawer knob above the sink, hang a mirror with a small chain, and voila!

3 Focus on the commode

    a. General rule: Place a picture above the toilet if possible. The picture should not be more than 20 inches above the toilet.

    b. The picture should be bold if the powder room has neutral-colored walls and should complement the flowers chosen. Or if the colors of the walls are bold, select a black and white picture that complements the flowers and other elements of the room.

    c. On top of the toilet, put folded towels and a plant or candle next to the towels. Make sure the smooth edge of the towels is facing out rather than the edges.

    d. Towels should be bold and should go well with the picture and the flowers.

4 Focus on towel holders

    a. If there is a rod, use a bigger towel and a hand towel on top of it. If there is just a hand towel ring, use only a hand towel.

5 Extra tips

    a. Always put the toilet seat down.

Dining Room/ Dinette

Items	Have Item	Purchase Item
4 chargers		
4 wine glasses		
4 plates (off-white usually)		
4 napkin rings		
4 napkins		
1 large centerpiece- usually a larger vase with monochromatic florals, which provides a dramatic look		
Silverware		
2 candle holders with candles or small mercury votives sprinkled randomly		
Artwork (large picture or set of 2 or 3)		
Rods & sheer curtains, if appropriate		

1

Put the table and four chairs centered under the light fixture. I usually use a round, glass table with decorative chairs.

2

Take a runner or square material and bend or scrunch it on the table.

237

3   Place the centerpiece underneath the light fixture.

4   Place the four chargers and plates on the table, and then add silverware.

5   Place the wine glasses over the knife and spoon on the right side of the plate.

6 Fold the napkins (see my YouTube video on how to fold napkins at **https://www. youtube.com/watch?v=unWFXmPVRdY**), and place it on the plate.

7 Add two candleholders with candles across from each other on the table, or randomly place five or seven votive holders on the table.

8 Choose the wall or walls for artwork seen while entering the room so that you have maximum impact to the buyer as they walk through the house for the first time.

Master and Full Bathrooms

Items	Have Item	Purchase Item
Large floral, monochromatic (with or without twigs)		
5 or more bath towels and 5 or more hand towels		
2 or more lanterns (different sizes)		
2 candlesticks with candles for large tub with a deck		
2-3 ivy plants or greenery		
5 or more small votive candles		
Bar of soap for tub		
Decorative pillows for deck of tub, if there is space		
2-3 pictures, I often use black and white		
Sheer curtain for shower with no shower doors		

1 Decide on color scheme, and use towels and florals that coordinate.

2 Place large florals between the sinks or on one side of the sink.

3 Fold two bath towels in thirds lengthwise and fold over the towel bar; fold a hand towel over the middle of the two bath towels.

4 Place hand towels over any small towel holder (circle ones are most common).

5 Consider hand towels placed at an angle next to the sink if it's a large space, or drape over each double sink if there is limited space beside the basin.

6 If there is a tub, fold one bath towel with a hand towel over it over the center of the tub side. Add a decorative bar of soap on top in the center for an added touch.

7 If there is a large deck on a tub or jacuzzi tub, in one corner, place a candle holder or two at different heights, and place an ivy in the middle of them to soften the look. Also, you can place two pillows in a corner with a lantern or decorative large votive at the opposite corner to add color and softness and to tie into the adjoining bedroom décor.

8 In the shower, I often place two bath towels on the deck or set and add the small glass candles in the soap tray or on the ledge in groups of three.

9 If the shower is part of the bathtub or without a shower door, I use a sheer curtain to the side with a shower rod to create a soft look and add elegance to the bathroom.

10 If there is space on the counter next to the floral, you can add lanterns or candle holders to create additional décor. I have also added a tray with a bottle of champagne and champagne glasses to add romance to the bathroom and to help it look luxurious.

242

11 For the toilet, you can fold two hand towels in a square with a ribbon and center it on the back of the toilet, or place a nice plant then add a picture not more than 12 inches above the toilet top in most cases.

12 If there is a wall behind the tub, that is a nice place to add a picture; if not, look for any other wall space to add art. Sometimes over a towel bar works really well.

13 If there is a window above the tub in the bathroom, I like to add sheer curtains with an iron rod and either puddle the curtains in the deck or use the 63" curtains. This add so much to the look of the bathroom!

14 An important tip to remember about master bathrooms: This is a room that you want to look as high end as possible, and buyers have a romantic idea of how they will soak in the tub sipping champagne, etc., so you want to help them see this room as the place where they can relax and have their home be that haven they desire.

Master Bedroom

Items	Have Item	Purchase Item
2-3 lamps		
Books		
Tall floral		
Wine glasses		
2 ivy plants or greenery		
Apples		
Afghan		
2 Candle holders		
2 Shams		
2 Larger pillows		
3-7 décor or accent color pillows		
1 Comforter		
2 chairs, if room for seating area		
2-3 end tables (or wooden tv trays)		
1-2 lanterns		
Inspirational wood sign or small picture		
1-2 artwork pieces for walls		

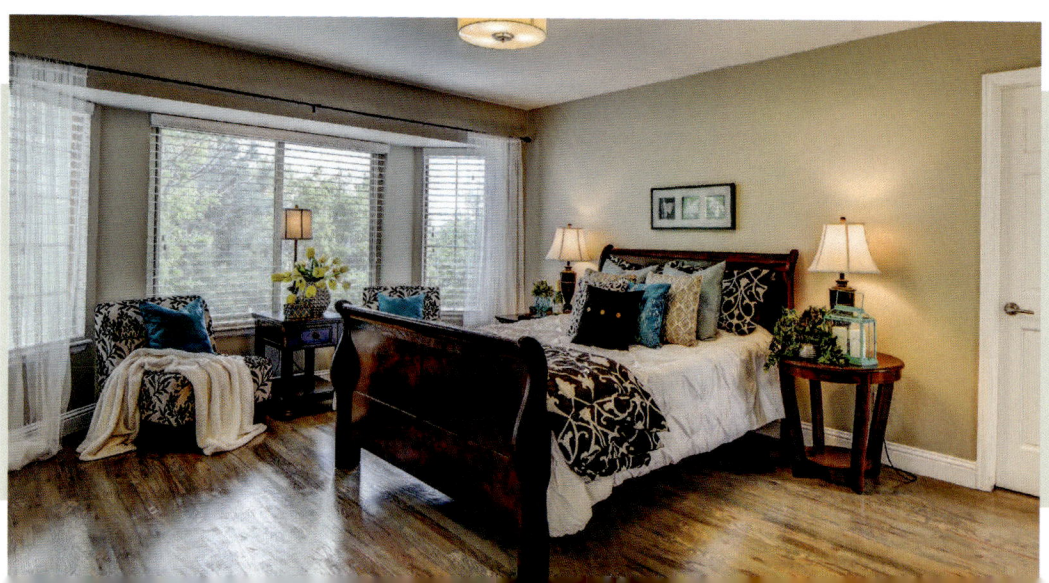

1 In a larger bedroom, I usually put the bed at an angle like this:

In a smaller bedroom, it probably has to go against a wall that is set up with outlets.

2 Place the end tables next to the bed. Include a lamp and groups of three with one side to include a taller floral.

3 I usually do three layers of pillows on the bed in addition to the shams (two shams, then two larger pillows, then two normal-sized pillows, then a décor pillow).

4 I always add iron rods and sheer curtains to the master bedroom. Imagine making it airy and relaxing—the curtains help. It makes it look clean, too!

5 If in an existing home, always remove personal photos from this room in particular!

6 Place the afghan at an angle draping over the end of the bed; make it look like it was tossed on the bed. This makes it seem like it is less "staged" and creates a relaxing feel to the room.

7

Place artwork over the headboard in rooms where you have to put the bed against the wall or to one side of the bed close to the end tables when the bed is at an angle. The main thing is that the picture is close enough to the bed to make it look like it all goes together, and the buyer can take it all in as soon as they walk or look into the room.

Congratulations!

You have completed Karen's 7-Second Home Selling System® from the book *7 Seconds, The 7 Second Rule: Why Your House Is Not Selling.*

You can continue to receive more information from Karen Conrad online!

Subscribe & receive MORE tips & tricks from Karen at

www.KarenConradHome.com

to help you on your home selling and staging journey!